Community Participation in School Management

Nobody denies that trust in schools is key to success in generating any educational outcomes. However, trust is often eroded, resulting in conflicts, alienation, and differentiation among school-level stakeholders. This book analyzes school-based management (SBM) of education through the lens of relational trust in the context of Ghana, revealing how community participation in school management leads to educational outcomes.

Conducting quantitative analysis of headteacher questionnaires from public basic schools and qualitative analysis of case study schools in the Akatsi South District of Ghana, Shibuya offers critical insights into building sustainable relationships between individual households and geographical/ school communities. He argues it is critical to highlight relational trust as an analytical tool to examine relationships between actors and factors in school management. The research finds that trust in schools is a two-way mechanism, and the mutuality of expectations and obligations among stakeholders is essential if children's learning outcomes are to improve.

With its mixed-methods approach, this book will be a valuable resource for scholars in comparative education, those in educational development, and those interested in African contexts.

Kazuro Shibuya is a director, Partnership Program Division, Chugoku Center, Japan International Cooperation Agency (JICA). He received his PhD in education from Hiroshima University, Japan, and his MA in education and economics program from Teachers College, Columbia University, USA.

Routledge Research in International and Comparative Education

This is a series that offers a global platform to engage scholars in continuous academic debate on key challenges and the latest thinking on issues in the fast-growing field of International and Comparative Education.

Titles in the series include:

European Perspectives on Inclusive Education in Canada
Critical Comparative Insights
Theodore Michael Christou, Robert Kruschel, Ian Alexander Matheson, and Kerstin Merz-Atalik

Globalization, Privatization, and Theories of State
Contemporary Education Reform in Honduras
D. Brent Edwards Jr., Mauro C. Moschetti, and Alejandro Caravaca

Configurations of Interdisciplinarity Within Education
Danish Experiences in a Global Educational Space
Trine Øland, Sofie Sauzet, Marie Larsen Ryberg, Katrine Lindvig

Learner-Centred Pedagogy in the Global South
Pupils and Teachers' Experiences
Nozomi Sakata

Community Participation in School Management
Relational Trust and Educational Outcomes
Kazuro Shibuya

For more information about this series, please visit: www.routledge.com/ Routledge-Research-in-International-and-Comparative-Education/ book-series/RRICE

Community Participation in School Management

Relational Trust and Educational Outcomes

Kazuro Shibuya

Routledge
Taylor & Francis Group

LONDON AND NEW YORK

First published 2023
by Routledge
4 Park Square, Milton Park, Abingdon, Oxon OX14 4RN

and by Routledge
605 Third Avenue, New York, NY 10158

Routledge is an imprint of the Taylor & Francis Group, an informa business

British Library Cataloguing-in-Publication Data
A catalogue record for this book is available from the British Library

Library of Congress Cataloging-in-Publication Data
Names: Shibuya, Kazuro, author.
Title: Community participation in school management : relational trust and educational outcomes / Kazuro Shibuya.
Description: Abingdon, Oxon ; New York, NY : Routledge, 2023. | Series: Routledge research in international and comparative education | Includes bibliographical references and index.
Identifiers: LCCN 2022024736 (print) | LCCN 2022024737 (ebook) | ISBN 9781032341026 (hardback) | ISBN 9781032341033 (paperback) | ISBN 9781003320579 (ebook)
Subjects: LCSH: School management and organization—Ghana. | Community and school—Ghana. | Educational leadership—Ghana.
Classification: LCC LB2970.G4 S55 2022 (print) | LCC LB2970.G4 (ebook) | DDC 371.2009667—dc23/eng/20220623
LC record available at https://lccn.loc.gov/2022024736
LC ebook record available at https://lccn.loc.gov/2022024737

ISBN: 978-1-032-34102-6 (hbk)
ISBN: 978-1-032-34103-3 (pbk)
ISBN: 978-1-003-32057-9 (ebk)

DOI: 10.4324/9781003320579

Typeset in Times New Roman
by Apex CoVantage, LLC

Contents

Illustrations

Tables

Figures

Foreword

The effort to provide quality education in global south contexts has often centered on the inputs from national governments as well as the contributions of international development agencies. More recently, however, the importance of local communities in promoting sustainable improvements in educational provision has been recognized. Although a lot has been written about how that can be achieved, this important book provides a unique and insightful theoretical and practical analysis on why community participation in school management holds the key to authentic school improvement in the African context.

Community participation in African schools has been extensively researched but remains a vexed issue, particularly when it comes to community participation in school management. Especially in African education systems, we know that school–community relations can be highly asymmetrical with communities often lacking real power to engage schools in ways that can bring about concrete improvements in educational outcomes.

The most prominent community participation in schools as research indicates is at the level of providing financial or human resources. This leaves communities in a subordinate role unable to participate in the kind of management decisions that can hold schools accountable to parents and communities. Participation is often based on schools' terms and their governing bodies, meaning communities' own interest and concerns remain at the periphery of schools' improvement agenda. Besides, the policy literature on community participation continues to place emphasis on building capacity and misses out completely on the fact that knowing why and how to engage with schools does nothing to address the power dynamics and trust issues, which are the real barriers to equitable and meaningful participation. Relational trust is the most difficult to achieve because often schools and their governing boards only pay lip service to communities and show little commitment to the community's own interests and concerns, especially regarding children's learning and achievement.

How can community members, caregivers/parents, headteachers, and teachers enter a school management relationship based on mutual expectations and obligations? How can poor rural communities play an equitable role in school management and feel a sense of empowerment that transcends tokenistic engagement? How can community members often with limited education hold teachers and headteachers accountable when it comes to children's learning? In fact, is effective participation in school management even possible when poor rural communities lack the social, economic, and educational capital to engage equitably? These are questions that the book raises and adequately addresses.

An erosion of trust between local communities and schools has resulted from years of unaccountable school governance. But as this book argues, trust is a two-way affair and essential for mutual accountability. Mutual expectations and obligations are essential if relational trust is to be realized. This book argues on the back of empirical evidence that we need to understand how synchronies of mutual expectations and obligations emerge to become reciprocal dynamics that make community participation in school management effective. Furthermore, the book unpacks the critical dynamic relationships between parents, children and teachers, and school communities, children, and schools. It goes on to provide empirical evidence to support the claim that "Teacher–parent relational trust is correlated with the results of Ghanaian basic education certification examinations." This is an important contribution to the scholarly literature on school–community relations in the sub-Saharan African context because it shows empirically that if relational trust can be improved, this can have a direct impact on learning outcomes. In addition, collective participation from communities can produce the necessary environment or factors that can lead to improvements in educational performance at school and child levels.

The book provides in-depth case study analysis to show that the realization of relational trust in the "Parent, school, community ties" can affect the realization of relational trust in other factors to either produce success or failure in the achievement of educational outcomes. But mutual accountability has two legs: school communities must be accountable to schools for providing support in the same way school communities have expectations for schools to provide quality education. This mutuality of expectations and obligations is essential if children's learning outcomes are to improve.

The book ends by discussing some key implications for the system of community participation in school management. Essentially, the need to formulate relational trust by matching capable headteachers with supportive school communities, the importance of ensuring mutual accountability involving key education stakeholders, making children and their learning the center of relational trust building at collective and individual levels, and finally providing support to fragile individuals and school communities to ensure the sustainability of relational trust.

This is a timely and important book that should be read by researchers, practitioners, and policy makers who are interested in understanding how to maximize community participation in school management to enhance the student learning experience and outcomes.

Kwame Akyeampong
Professor of International Education
and Development
The Open University, UK

Acknowledgment

This book has been developed based on a PhD thesis conferred by Hiroshima University, Japan. I am grateful to headteachers, teachers, and school communities who willingly participated in my case study through interviews and headteachers who provided responses to my questionnaires. I appreciate the Ghana Education Service for giving me the permission to conduct this study, especially Mr. Adovor Yogah, the District Director of Education, and Mr. Clements Katsekpor, the Director of Administration and Finance, Akatsi South District education office, who provided the needed support for me to conduct the field surveys. I really appreciate Mr. Clements' dedication to accompany my field surveys. He had a deeper understanding of the context in the field and provided me with rich information that encouraged me to complete this study.

Many thanks to Mr. Fred Birikorang and Ms. Junko Nakazawa, Basic Education Division, GES HQ, for their continuous support and inputs they provided for my research. I also appreciate precious suggestions by Dr. Stephen Adu, who is my former colleague at the Teacher Education Division, GES, and has written an important Ph.D. dissertation in the field of headteacher leadership and community participation in Ghana. He also supported me with English proofreading of the manuscript. I show my gratitude to the Ghana Statistical Service for providing me the Population and Housing Census 2010 data in Akatsi South District, which enabled me to calculate socioeconomic status data for school communities.

I am most grateful to Prof. Ayami Nakaya for her continuous support and encouragement. Her comments always encouraged me to do more to deepen discussions and contributions to theories and practices. I show my deep gratitude to Prof. Takuya Baba, who taught me academic rigors and logical sequence in the study. I also thank Prof. Kinya Shimizu for his support and advice to the quantitative analysis and Prof. Jun Takizawa for his advice to theoretical contribution of this study to the literature. I owe a lot of gratitude to Prof. Kwame Akyeampong for his comments as a Ghanaian who knows the context and an experienced African researcher in the field of education. He kindly accepted to write a foreword for this study. I appreciate his generous contribution to shedding more light on the significance of my academic work.

I show my appreciation to Prof. Shoko Yamada, who invited me to join a research group to study "African Potentials," which sponsored part of my field surveys (JSPS Kakenhi Grant Number JP16H06318). I have received precious advice from discussions with this research group, which helped me to analyze issues from multifaceted perspectives in an African context. I also express my gratitude to Prof. Mikiko Nishimura for holding a joint session at the Comparative and International Education Society (CIES) 2018 Annual Conference in the Mexico City and inviting me to contribute a book chapter in this field. I thank the JSPS Kakenhi Grant Number 17K04627 for sponsoring most of my field surveys and academic work. I also appreciate Katie Peace and Kendrick Loo of Tayor & Francis who supported me to complete this book.

Finally, I would like to show sincere appreciation to my wife, Mia, and my children, Takashi, Atsushi, and Yui, for their understanding, patience, and encouragement to my academic work. I also thank my mother, Keiko, for her continuous support. I dedicate this study to all my family, including my late father, Makoto Shibuya.

Abbreviations

BECE	Basic Education Certificate Examination
DA	District Assembly
EMIS	Education Management Information System
fCUBE	Free, Compulsory, Universal, Basic Education
GES	Ghana Education Service
GSS	Ghana Statistical Service
JHS	Junior High School
KG	Kindergarten
PTA	Parent Teacher Association
RT	Relational Trust
SBM	School-Based Management
SES	Socioeconomic Status
SHS	Senior High School
SMC	School Management Committee
SPAM	School Performance Appraisal Meeting
SPIP	School Performance Improvement Plan

1 Why does community participation in school management matter?

Background

Community support for education has a long history worldwide. According to Hoppers (2005) who studied community school initiatives in Africa, on the one hand, community school programs arose from the need for an adaptive response to the absence of or poor access to mainstream educational provisions. On the other hand, transformative response represents the perspective that education can contribute to social change through empowering learners to gain an understanding of and control over social, economic, and/or political forces.

In Africa, indigenous geographical communities established and supported schools even before independence, until the 1960s and 1970s when governments established their own schools. Schools established by the self-help community development in Eastern Africa are examples of adaptive responses that provided educational alternatives to mainstream public education offered by the government (Bamattre, 2019; Hoppers, 2005; Nishimura, 2017; Yamada, 2014). Decentralization policies in various countries since the 1990s had pushed for such community school initiatives. On the contrary, in community schools with transformative responses, stakeholders are expected to practice democratic participation by raising their voices in education for transformation. That includes cases that the politically marginalized or the poor aimed for a school curriculum that is designed with emphasis on their community empowerment (Tarlau, 2019; Edwards, 2019). Rationales for decentralization and democratization are not binary but exist in a mixed manner within the respective community school initiatives (Clothely & Heidemann, 2019).

In the 1990s, various African countries introduced Universal Primary Education policies and abolished school fees, which implied that governments provided free public education. However, along the line, many governments faced severe resource scarcity and could not support the free

DOI: 10.4324/9781003320579-1

public education with expanded access to schooling. As such, community participation in school management was considered as an appropriate instrumental approach to bringing about educational outcomes and has been institutionalized as a form of school-based management (SBM) approach in the context of decentralization (Barrera-Osorio et al., 2009; Bruns et al., 2011; De Grauwe, 2005).

In Ghana, where the author conducted this research, geographical communities under the traditional chieftaincy institutions took the initiative to establish and support schools as part of community development in the absence of or lack of government support. The government then gradually absorbed such community schools, registered them as public schools, and deployed teachers to teach in these schools. The management and control of the schools thus shifted to central government authorities, and communities tended to be less actively involved (Essuman, 2013). In that sense, though the generalization is not possible, the case of Ghana seems to shed more light on the characteristics of community school initiatives with adaptive responses.

Statement of problems

As stated above, literature have aimed to reveal how schools can achieve educational outcomes. School effectiveness/improvement studies have identified the characteristics/factors of school management that can generate educational outcomes. However, there still exist research gaps regarding how to link managerial and pedagogical factors toward educational outcome (Bossert, 1988). It is also challenging how to activate these factors in developing countries under severe resource scarcity (Lockheed & Levin, 1993).

Geographical community members and guardians have supported school development since their establishment. Decentralization reforms in education have institutionalized community/parent participation in school management and have formulated SBM teams concerned with pupils' education. Thus, the involvement of geographical communities and guardians in schools has changed from supporting school development to them participating in school management and holding schools accountable. However, there have been mixed results in terms of the effects of SBM on educational outcomes (Edwards & Loucel, 2016; Nishimura, 2017; Snilstveit et al., 2015; Yamada, 2014). Moreover, various conflicts, mistrust, alienation, and differentiation have been observed among school-level stakeholders (Carney et al., 2007; Essuman & Akyeampong, 2011; Pellini, 2005). Therefore, it is an important research gap in theoretical and practical perspectives to identify how community participation in school management can manage relationships among school-level stakeholders that would lead to educational outcomes.

Various attempts have been made to mitigate such complex relationships among school-level stakeholders. These includes reciprocal relationship (Essuman & Akyeampong, 2011), mutual accountability (Nishimura, 2017), two-way communication (Adu, 2016; Epstein et al., 2002), social capital (Edwards, 2019; Pryor, 2005), and relational trust (RT). RT is a concept proposed by Bryk and Schneider (2002) who believe that it fits the analysis of schooling characterized by interdependency. However, how to generate such relationships among school-level stakeholders regarding factors of school management to improve educational outcomes remains unknown.

Research objectives

The objective of this study is to reveal how community participation in school management leads to educational outcomes, based on the perspective of RT.

Research questions

1) To what extent does community participation function in school management?
2) To what extent are community participation, socioeconomic status (SES), educational outcomes, and RT related?
3) How is RT realized between actors and factors of school management to generate educational outcomes?

Significance of the study

This study is significant for the following reasons. First, this study aims to address how factors, actors, and their relationship in school management can be connected through the concept of RT. This study can provide insights into how one can achieve educational outcomes by influencing factors and actors in school management through realizing RT. In particular, pupils' discipline or pupils' motivation for learning is critical because pupils are the subject of learning and they must be motivated or encouraged to learn by school communities, teachers, and guardians to improve educational outcomes.

Second, this study is significant in that it considers the relationships between collectives of community and individual households in a contemporary era where economical and educational disparities have expanded. Affluent households may leave their geographical communities to look for quality schools for their children as they are able to choose schools based on their own preferences. However, fragile households may be left behind in marginalized communities in low-income countries owing to their low SES. Thus, it is critical to determine how they can achieve educational outcomes despite low SES through collaborative efforts in the collective space of the communities.

Research context

Ghana has a history of both indigenous and institutionalized community participation in school management. Ghana introduced policies and practices of community participation in education relatively earlier compared to other West African countries. Thus, I chose Ghana, as various lessons from past interventions can be extracted and shared with neighboring countries, which are currently accelerating policies and practices in this field.

I chose the Akatsi South District in the Volta Region in Ghana as the field of study. This district has been selected as one of the pilot districts for the Japan International Cooperation Agency (JICA)-supported community participation interventions. I selected this district because the District Director of Education was committed to implementing the pilot activity and also showed interest in supporting my research related to this topic. This guaranteed my ability to obtain a satisfactory level of cooperation from the district education office for the research. I visited schools that were not selected as targets by the pilot activity to avoid any influence of the intervention on the research to the largest extent possible.

In terms of mean annual per capita income, the Volta Region ranked fourth among the ten regions in Ghana (Ghana Statistical Service, 2014). The Akatsi South District is not one of the deprived districts as it has better poverty indicators among other districts. The major ethnic group in the district is the Ewe, which is dominant in the Volta Region. In 2013, the Akatsi South District was positioned 18th among the 25 districts in the Volta Region in terms of the Basic Education Certificate Examination (BECE) pass rate ranking. As of September 2017, the district had 107 basic schools, comprising 84 public schools (kindergarten [KG]-75; primary-70; junior high school (JHS)-40) and 23 private basic schools. The district capital, Akatsi, is located approximately 140 km from the national capital, Accra, making it very convenient to travel to and from Accra.

References

Adu, S. (2016). *The role of headteacher leadership and community participation in public school improvement in Ghana* [Unpublished doctoral dissertation, University of Sussex].

Bamattre, R. (2019). Between state and society: Community schools in Zambia. In R. Clothey & K. Heidemann (Eds.), *Another way: Decentralization, democratization, and the global politics of community-based schooling* (pp. 97–113). Brill Sense.

Barrera-Osorio, F., Tazeen, F., Patrinos, H. A., & Santibáñez, L. (2009). *Decentralized decision-making in schools: The theory and evidence on school cased management*. World Bank.

Bossert, S. (1988). School effects. In N. Boyan (Ed.), *The handbook of research on educational administration* (pp. 341–354). Longman.

Bruns, B., Deon, F., & Harry, A. P. (2011). *Making schools work: New evidence on accountability reforms*. World Bank.

Bryk, A. S., & Schneider, B. (2002). *Trust in schools: A core resource for improvement*. Russell Sage Foundation.

Carney, S., Bista, M., & Agergaard, J. (2007). Empowering the local through education? Exploring community-managed schooling in Nepal. *Oxford Review of Education, 33*(5), 611–628.

Clothey, R., & Heidemann, K. (2019). *Another way: Decentralization, democratization, and the global politics of community-based schooling*. Brill Sense.

De Grauwe, A. (2005). Improving the quality of education through school based management: Learning from international experiences. *International Review of Education, 51*(4), 269–287.

Edwards Jr., D. B. (2019). Shifting the perspective on community-based management of education: From systems theory to social capital and community empowerment. *International Journal of Educational Development, 64*, 17–26.

Edwards Jr., D. B. (2019). Accountability through community-based management? Implications from the local level implementation in El Salvador of a globally popular model. In R. Clothey & K. Heidemann (Eds.), *Another way: Decentralization, democratization, and the global politics of community-based schooling* (pp. 47–64). Brill Sense.

Edwards Jr., D. B., & Loucel, C. (2016). The EDUCO program, impact evaluations, and the political economy of global education reform. *Education Policy Analysis Archives, 24*(92), 1–46.

Epstein, J. L., Sanders, M. G., Simon, B. S., Salinas, K. C., Jansorn, N. R., & Van Voorhis, F. L. (2002). *School, family, and community partnerships: Your handbook for action* (2nd ed.). Corwin Press Inc., A Sage Publications Company.

Essuman, A. (2013). *Decentralization of education management in Ghana: Key issues in school-community relations*. LAP LAMBERT Academic Publishing.

Essuman, A., & Akyeampong, K. (2011). Decentralisation policy and practice in Ghana: The promise and reality of community participation in education in rural community. *Journal of Education Policy, 26*(4), 513–527.

Ghana Statistical Service. (2014). *Population and housing census: District analytical report Akatsi South district*. Retrieved November 22, 2018, from www.statsghana.gov.gh/docfiles/2010_District_Report/Volta/AKATSI%20SOUTH.pdf

Hoppers, W. (2005). Community schools as an educational alternative in Africa: A critique. *International Review of Education, 51*(2–3), 115–137.

Lockheed, M. E., & Levin, H. M. (1993). Creating effective schools. In H. M. Levin & M. E. Lockheed (Eds.), *Effective schools in developing countries*. The Falmer Press.

Nishimura, M. (2017). Community participation in school management in developing countries. *Oxford Research Encyclopedia of Education*. https://doi.org/10.1093/acrefore/9780190264093.013.64

Pellini, A. (2005). Decentralization of education in Cambodia: Searching for spaces of participation between traditions and modernity. *Compare, 35*(2), 205–216.

Pryor, J. (2005). Can community participation mobilize social capital for improvement of rural schooling? A case study from Ghana. *Compare, 35*(2), 193–203.

Snilstveit, B., Stevenson, J., Phillips, D., Vojtkova, M., Gallagher, E., Schmidt, T., Jobse, H., Geelen, M., Pastorello, M., & Eyers, J. (2015). *Interventions for improving learning outcomes and access to education in low- and middle- income countries: A systematic review, 3ie systematic review, 24*. International Initiative for Impact Evaluation (3ie).

Tarlau, R. (2019). Social movement-led democratic governance of public education: The case of the Brazilian landless workers movement. In R. Clothey & K. Heidemann (Eds.), *Another way: Decentralization, democratization, and the global politics of community-based schooling* (pp. 11–30). Brill Sense.

Yamada, S. (2014). Determinants of 'community participation': The tradition of local initiatives and the institutionalization of school management committees in Oromia Region, Ethiopia. *Compare, 44*(2), 162–185.

2   Factors and actors
in school management

Introduction

Chapter 1 describes the problem statement regarding community participation in school management and presents the research objectives, the significance of the research, and the structure of this study. This chapter reviews the literature on school management in the following areas of studies related to school management: school effectiveness studies, school improvement studies, and school-based management studies. First, it starts with the fundamental arguments between SES, educational outcomes, and school management. Second, by reviewing the school management literature, this chapter discusses the following topics: factors and actors in school management; participation, accountability, leadership, and social capital as underlying theories in school management. To understand the process of school management to yield educational outcomes and how to manage conflicts among school communities, this chapter pays attention to the concept of RT, which is composed of the synchronies of mutual expectations and obligations among community members, guardians, headteachers, and teachers.

Educational outcomes and school management

Educational outcomes

School effectiveness studies have argued over the definition of "school effects," that is, the educational outcomes of schooling. There are multiple goals attached to schools as social agencies (Bossert, 1988). The cognitive aspects of learning, namely, to learn reading, writing, and arithmetic, are often regarded as the key "effect" to educational outcomes. However, what is treated as an "effect" in one study may be viewed as a factor that produces effects in another study (Bossert, 1988). This suggests that school effects may differ depending on the values attached to schooling and implies that several school effects exist in a complicated structure. Epstein et al. (2002)

DOI: 10.4324/9781003320579-2

emphasized that if children feel cared for and are encouraged to work hard in their role as a student, they are more likely to do their best to learn to read, write, calculate, and learn other skills and talents and to remain in school. Fertig (2000) argued that schools should be allowed to set their own educational goals. Thus, it appears to be necessary to view "school effects" from several perspectives, rather than being limited to learning outcomes measured by test scores.

SES and educational outcomes

SES is defined using the following information, which represents the social and economic situation of each individual or the members in a household: level of educational attainment, income, and occupation. In 1966, the Coleman Report revealed that households' SES is more likely to determine pupils' learning outcomes than school factors. The report aimed to document the availability of equal educational opportunities among white majority pupils and ethnic minority pupils. The report found that the schools were remarkably similar in the way they related to the achievement of their pupils when the socioeconomic background of their students was considered. The average white student's achievements appeared to be less affected by the strength or weakness of their school's facilities, curricula, and teachers than the average minority pupil's achievements. In other words, the achievements of minority pupils were found to be more dependent on the schools they attended than those of white majority pupils (Coleman et al., 1966). Although the intention of the report was to reveal the availability of equal educational opportunities between white pupils and minority pupils, it was interpreted as showing that the SES of pupils' households matters more to their learning outcomes than school inputs.

Attention to school management studies

To refute the conclusion of the Coleman Report, many studies have focused on the argument that "schools make a difference." There are two streams of research in this area. On one hand, school effectiveness studies have aimed to answer the following question: What activities will have greater benefits for pupils? Studies in this area tend to focus on outcomes, the use of data for decision-making, and adoption of quantitative approaches to analyze school management. These studies often adopted the context-input-process-output model (Schreens, 1990; Yu, 2007). On the other hand, school improvement studies aim to answer the following question: How can we make our school better than it is now (Stoll, 1996)? School improvement studies tend to focus on the process, have an orientation toward actions, and analyze a strategy for educational changes that enhance student outcomes as well as strengthen schools' capacity to manage change from a qualitative viewpoint. Studies in this area also emphasize teacher involvement in efforts to enact changes and focuses on teaching and learning (Chapman & Sammons, 2013).

Factors in school management

School effectiveness and school improvement studies have identified both managerial and pedagogical factors in school management for producing educational outcomes. The main actors in school management are head-teachers and teachers, whereas parents and geographical community members are regarded as inputs for school management. The following literature reviews of school effectiveness and school improvement studies explain the managerial and pedagogical factors in school management.

Managerial factors

In school effectiveness studies, the organizational aspect of schooling is often highlighted and the context-input-process-output model is often considered (Schreens, 1990). The process of school management involves the following indicators, based on effective school studies: educational leadership; achievement-oriented policy; orderly and safe climate; clear objectives; high expectations; monitoring/evaluation of pupils' progress; continuity and consensus among teachers.

In the context of developing countries, Heneveld and Craig (1996) developed a conceptual framework including factors that determine school effectiveness. It identified two managerial factors: "School climate" (high expectations of students, positive attitude of teachers, order and discipline, organized curriculum, and rewards and incentives) and "Enabling conditions" (effective leadership, a capable teaching force, flexibility and autonomy, and high time-in-schools). Parent and community support were still regarded as supporting inputs and were positioned outside of school management.

Bryk et al. (2010) presented a framework containing the following managerial factors: "Leadership," "Professional Capacity," "School Learning Climate," and "Instructional Guidance." "Leadership" is regarded as the extent of the various kinds of leadership demonstrated by headteachers. "Professional Capacity" covers teacher orientation toward innovation and their school commitment. "Parent-Community-School Ties" refers to teacher outreach to parents and parents' involvement in the school and "School Learning Climate" includes safety and order in classrooms. In this framework, "Parent-Community-School Ties" is considered to be one of the managerial factors in school management, which implied that parents and community members are not just supporting inputs but are part of school management (Appendix 1).

Pedagogical factors

Schreens (1990) explained the following pedagogical process indicators within integrated model of school effectiveness at the school and classroom levels: effective learning time or "time on task," structured or "direct" teaching, and opportunities to learn or "content covered." Sammons et al. (1995) asserted that concentration on teaching and learning, purposeful teaching, and high expectations have the most significant role to play in fostering pupils' learning and progress and in influencing their educational outcomes. According to Bryk et al. (2010), pedagogical factors in school management comprise the following: the "Instructional Triangle," comprising the pupil, teacher, and subject matter; "Time for Learning"; "Supplementary Resources" as multiplier; and "Dynamics of Student Learning," which is composed of "Students' Motivation to Learn" and "Students' School Participation." "Students' Participation" includes regular attendance, a lack of tardiness, few discipline problems, and regular completion of homework.

In the context of developing countries, Lockheed and Verspoor (1991) also presented a model of educational effectiveness containing the following process factors related to pedagogical aspects: improving curriculum, providing learning materials, time for learning, effective teaching, and children's learning capacity. Lockheed and Levin (1993) articulated that curriculum, instructional materials, time for learning, and teaching practices are necessary inputs to promote student learning. Heneveld and Craig (1996) included "teaching/learning process (high learning time, variety in teaching strategies, frequent homework, frequent student assessment, and feedback)" in their conceptual framework as a pedagogical factor in school management.

Actors and underlying theories in school management

In both school effectiveness and school improvement studies, in-school factors, where headteachers and teachers are mostly engaged, have been emphasized as being critical, whereas community/parent support has often been regarded as one of the inputs. Bryk et al. (2010) regarded "Parent, School, Community Ties" to be inside school management. Thus, community/parent participation has shifted from being viewed as an input into school management to being one of its managerial factors. While teaching professionals are the critical agents of change in school effectiveness and school improvement studies, teachers in developing countries are fragile in terms of their low social status, which becomes difficult to depend on them for school improvement. Thus, it is critical in the context of developing countries to know how teachers/headteacher and parents/community members can collaborate with each other to improve educational outcomes.

Actors

Effective schools appear to have a high degree of school-level responsibilities and authorities, with accountability to parents and their local communities (Lockheed & Levin, 1993). Following the school effectiveness studies, SBM builds on the following theories: autonomy, participation, and accountability (Bruns et al., 2011). With the background of decentralization reforms, school-based management has been introduced as a way to delegate the decision-making authority to the school level (Bruns et al., 2011; Caldwell, 2005).

SBM programs include the following types: administrative control (headteachers-led), professional control (teachers-led), community control (community members and parents-led), and balanced control (Barrera-Osorio et al., 2009). Therefore, actors include headteachers, teachers, community members, parents, and any other members related to local education administration. SBM programs have different intentions depending on the context. In developed countries, it is intended to enhance teachers' professionalism because it allows teachers to design programs that meet the needs at the school level (Lockheed & Levin, 1993).

On the contrary, in developing countries, SBM programs with an emphasis on community or parent participation have spread out widely. Behind the scene, there have been serious concerns about teachers' absenteeism and lack of pupils' time-on-task. Thus, SBM programs in developing countries have been intended to make schools and teachers work through oversight from community members and parents. Community and parent representatives are expected to become members of school governing bodies, which form part of local educational administration. In this way, they make decisions on school management, oversee it, and hold schools and/or teachers accountable to them for school performance. The World Development Report 2004 highlighted that there was a short route of accountability between clients (community members and parents) and service providers (schools). Empirical evidence has also been accumulated to justify that SBM programs with emphasis on community/parent participation produce improved educational outcomes (Barrera-Osorio et al., 2009; Bruns et al., 2011). This has enabled SBM programs to spread out to various developing countries.

Community

"Community" appears frequently in the literature; however, its definition needs to be clarified. Community has been defined in the literature as follows: geographical community, cultural community, and school community (Bray, 2000; Nishimura, 2017; Rose, 2003; Taniguchi & Hirakawa, 2016). A geographical community refers to a group of people who reside in the same geographical boundary. A cultural community includes those who share the same religion, ethnic group, gender, and generation.

A school community denotes a group of people who work together for the purpose of school management, regardless of their geographical locations or cultural backgrounds. A school community is likely to overlap with geographical communities in the case of rural schools because guardians reside in geographical communities (Nishimura, 2017; Rose, 2003). Sergiovanni (1994) posited that a school community includes the faculties or staff of the school organization, as well as the school-level stakeholders, including parents, community members, and local organizations. Headteachers have dual positions in a school community as they lead the teaching force in daily school management and are engaged with wider stakeholders as a member of the school governing body.

Historically, there have been "community schools" in sub-Saharan Africa, which were established by geographical communities (Hoppers, 2005). However, literature have pointed out that geographical communities are not necessarily homogeneous and consensual to support the development of schools in geographical boundaries (Rose, 2003). There are multilayered communities that include geographical communities' members, virtual kinship network, age, gender-specific groups, and those who have enrolled children (Yamada, 2014). There are differences between those geographical communities nearby schools and those that are away from schools in terms of participation in school events (Saito, 2013). Immigration and the disintegration of matrilineal family structures have also affected the dispositions of rural people to schooling (Pryor, 2005).

As such, commonality between geographical and school communities has been dissolved. Geographical communities have established schools within their boundaries and guardians have sent their children to those schools. However, some guardians have tended to send their children to public or private schools in urban areas that can offer quality education. In such cases, they joined a new school community, though guardians were still members of the geographical communities. Thus, under such circumstances, geographical and school communities may not be the same and fragile households may be marginalized within such geographical communities, resulting in expanded educational and regional disparities (Edwards,

2019; Ogawa, 2017). Due to the expansion of school choice, households may join several school communities because their children attend different schools in or beyond geographical boundaries (Yamada, 2014).

Participation and associated theories

Participation

Participation is a buzzword in the field of development (Edwards & Klees, 2015). It is a complex term, which can be taken differently according to the setting and the rationale. The concept of participation is often intimately tied with the notion of community, which is also a contested term (Rose, 2003). Thus, I carefully reviewed who participated (subject) in what (object), to what extent (degree), how they did so (modality), and why they did so (rationale), based on the literature review.

In the literature regarding community participation in school management, it is community members and guardians who are the most common subjects of participation, as described earlier. They have supported schools since their establishment and have been regarded as the subject of the decision-making in school management. Headteachers and teachers are actually responsible for the day-to-day running of schools and are indispensable subjects of school management.

Pupils have rarely been discussed as the subject of participation in school management in the literature. However, in the case of Ethiopia, Mitchell (2017) paid attention to pupils' participation in school management, such as student leaders who provide academic support and behavioral control to their peers. In the literature regarding parents' involvement in education, Epstein et al. (2002) asserted that students are the main actors in their education, development, and success in school. Epstein et al. (2002) also stressed that partnership activities among families, schools, and communities can be designed to engage, guide, energize, and motivate students to achieve their own successes. These studies assumed that if children feel cared for, and are encouraged to study hard, they are more likely to do their best and continue to go to school. Sanders (2002) also articulated the significance of two-way communications between schools and community partners, stating that one simple measure to determine the level of appropriateness of the community partnership was to examine whether the partnership was positive for students.

In terms of the objects of participation, SBM programs transfer authority over budget (payment of teachers, mobilizing resources), personnel (teacher hiring/firing), pedagogy (curriculum development, teacher training, textbook design, and textbook distribution), maintenance and infrastructure, and monitoring and evaluation at the school level (Barrera-Osorio et al., 2009; Rose, 2003). The degree of participation ranges from the pseudo-participation to the genuine participation in the following order: use of service, contribution of resources, attendance at meetings, consultation on issues, involvement in delivery, and delegated powers and decision-making (Rose, 2003). Epstein et al. (2002) also classified parent involvement as follows: parenting, communicating, volunteering, learning at home, decision-making, and collaborating with the community.

The modality of participation is associated with the rationale of participation, the modality of community, and the organizational unit. Collective participation means that decision-making, resource mobilization, and information sharing are being conducted in a collective space. The participatory democracy is a key rationale for collective participation. However, its interpretation appears to be different in Western and African societies. On one hand, according to Bryk and Schneider (2002), in the context of Western society, Putnam (2000) emphasized the willingness of citizens to associate voluntarily with one another to redress collective concerns. On the other hand, under the context of African society, Nyamnjoh (2016) considered individuals to be incomplete, such that they formulate communities of interdependence. Yntiso et al. (2017) argued that the Western institutional setting focuses on individuals, whereas the African cultures consider the collectives to be the units of social organizations.

Within collective participation, on one hand, the elective representatives of community members and parents meet, discuss, and make decisions based on the principle of representative democracy in an institutionalized school community. On the other hand, as Yamada (2014) pointed out, even before the institutionalized school communities were established, indigenous geographical communities had met and discussed issues on education, based on the principle of consensual democracy in African society (Ajei, 2001).

Representative democracy builds on several rationales. The first rationale is the legitimacy of participation. Teaching professionals have dominated decision-making in schools; however, community members, including parents, participate in school management as democratic institutions. The second rationale is the effectiveness of participation. It assumed that if decision-making authorities are delegated to the school level, it becomes possible to respond to schools' needs effectively (Welsh & McGinn, 1999) and is likely to produce educational outcomes effectively. This kind of notion is called an instrumental approach toward participation (Edwards & Klees, 2015) because participation becomes a powerful instrument for community members and guardians to demand accountability for schools.

School governing bodies and parent voluntary organizations are tangible forms of institutionalized participation. School governing bodies often

Table 2.1 Correspondence between the modality and the rationale of participation, modality of community, and organizational unit

Modality of participation	Rationale of participation			Modality of community	Organizational unit
Collective participation	Participatory democracy (Putnam, 2000) Indirect participation (Suzuki, 2002); social relationship at institutional level (Epstein et al., 2002)	Representative democracy (Edwards & Klees, 2015)	Legitimacy, democracy, effectiveness; (Welsh & McGinn, 1999); instrumental approach (Edwards & Klees, 2015); parents as decision-makers (Martiniello, 2000)	Institutionalized school communities (Yamada, 2014)	School governing body (executive meeting)
			Collaboration and mutual support for pupils' education (volunteering, collaboration with community) (Epstein et al., 2002); parents as providers of support for the school (Martiniello, 2000)		Parent association/ PTA (general meeting)
		Consensual democracy (Ajei, 2001)	Collaboration and mutual support for community development (Ajei, 2001)	Indigenous geographical communities (Yamada, 2014)	Town/village/ community assembly
Individual participation	Direct participation (Suzuki, 2002); social relationship at individual level (Epstein et al., 2002)	Parenting, communicating, learning at home (Epstein, 2002; Carolan-Silva, 2011; Suzuki, 2002)	Parents as responsible for child rearing, parents as co-teachers (Martiniello, 2000)		Household/ home
		School choice (Suzuki, 2002)	Efficiency and effectiveness		

place more emphasis on representative democracy in terms of the decision-making of school management, while parent voluntary organizations build on the consensual democracy rationale, which embraces collaboration and mutual support for their children's education.

On the contrary to collective participation, individual participation deals with rearing one's own children according to an individual household's goals. This involves direct engagement with children as it relates to daily rearing at home. Parent participation in children's learning has been shown to be the most effective form of parent involvement for improving learning outcomes (Martiniello, 2000). However, in developing countries, guardians in rural areas tend to prefer collective participation (attending school meetings) to individual participation (looking after children's homework at home) due to their low educational background (Carolan-Silva, 2011).

Parent participation includes both collective or indirect, and individual or direct participation (Carolan-Silva, 2011; Epstein et al., 2002; Suzuki, 2002). When parents volunteer, make decisions, and collaborate, this appears to be part of indirect engagement with children and collective participation as school communities. On the other hand, when parents communicate with individual teachers and children and make sure that children are cared for and learn at home, this appears to be more similar to direct engagement with children and individual participation. Community participation and parent participation are often referred to interchangeably, but based on perspective of collective and individual participation, they can be distinguished accordingly.

Community participation in school management has changed the positions of both community members and parents in relation to schools. In the past, they tended to be viewed as inputs into school management or as supporters of school development as members of geographical communities. They have been engaged with their children in rearing and supporting them to learn at home as parents. However, with the introduction of the institutionalized mechanism, community/parent representatives have become decision-makers in school management. This has created various challenges in the relationships among school-level stakeholders. Such challenges include: when the elite capture the notion that a few stakeholders dominate the decision-making processes (Pellini, 2005; Saito, 2013); information asymmetry between teachers and parents over pedagogical issues (Suzuki, 2002); lack of knowledge, skills, and the will for communities to manage schools (Carolan-Silva, 2011; Mfum-Mensah & Friedson-Ridenour, 2014; Chapman et al., 2002); lack of time for poor parents to engage in school management (Cuellar-Marchelli, 2003); parents' invasion of teachers' professional autonomy; and cost of participation (Carney et al., 2007; Essuman & Akyeampong, 2011).

Participation and accountability

The introduction of participation discourse has been accompanied by the theory of accountability (Suzuki, 2002). The World Development Report 2004 stressed that citizens, including parents and community members, are clients who can exercise their power to service providers in the education sector (World Bank, 2003). In this regard, parents and community members have become the subjects who participate in school management as well as demand accountability from school management.

There are several assumptions that we tend to overlook in the accountability framework presented by the World Bank. First, it is assumed that if community members and parents participate in school management, then schools are held accountable to them for school performance. It assumes that strengthening managerial approaches to make communities and parents supervise teachers would make teachers feel obliged to come to schools on time and deliver their expected services (World Bank, 2003). However, the literature review shows that the SBM studies have not addressed the prevailing theoretical challenges in school management regarding the linkages between managerial and pedagogical factors toward educational outcomes. Edwards (2019) argued that an SBM program in El Salvador was heavily weighted toward managerial aspects and did not sufficiently address pedagogical aspects. Other studies have criticized the one-way participation–accountability framework as an instrumental approach to community participation for educational outcomes (Edwards & Klees, 2015; Nishimura, 2018). This is especially critical in the context of developing countries, which may experience severe resource scarcity. Okitsu and Edwards (2017) argued that teachers' own survival needs, such as their livelihoods and ways of commuting, trumped their sense of obligations or accountability to parents or the community.

Second, it is assumed that both long-route and short-route accountability work in tandem in the conceptual framework. However, the long-route accountability appears to have less attention in practice. This is particularly true regarding support from the central government or local government/ education offices to educational service providers. However, as Gershberg et al. (2012) described, there are various government responsibilities in long-route accountability. For instance, the subnational level of government or management is supposed to conduct the following for the sake of educational service providers: communicate, explain, monitor, evaluate, and/ or enforce norms and standards; distribute educational resources, supervise and support schools, and conduct human resource management. Thus, as Essuman (2013) pointed out, schools did not believe that they were accountable to school communities, rather they feel accountable to the education directorate. However, in reality, delays in the capitation grant from the government have made it impossible for schools to be held accountable for their performance (Adu, 2016; Malakolunthu et al., 2014). De Grauwe (2005) argued that underperforming schools need support more than they need accountability. This means that poorly performing schools need internal capacity building or advice on how to improve before holding themselves accountable externally. Under such circumstances, government's responsibilities are to support and monitor fragile school communities and schools.

Based on this conceptual framework of accountability, the institutionalized mechanism of community participation in school management has been spread out worldwide and has been supported by various development partners (Barrera-Osorio et al., 2009). For instance, the World Bank found that 17 percentage of its education sector projects between 2003 and 2013 had components addressing school autonomy and accountability (Takeda et al., 2013). The Project Appraisal Document for the World Bank Project in Senegal, stated that the impact evaluation results supported the positive effects of school-based management interventions (establishment of School Management Committee [SMC], training of stakeholders, development of the School Performance Improvement Plan [SPIP], etc.) on student test scores (World Bank, 2013). This document clearly stated that "the percentage of schools with functional School Management Committees" is one of the critical indicators without specifying what they mean.

Participation and leadership

Yamada (2014) argued that one of the major factors that divide active and inactive schools is leadership. According to Yamada (2014), leadership in community participation in school management can take several forms. The first is the leaders who hold a certain level of administrative authority in traditional organizations. This type of leadership has been available even before the institutionalized mechanism of community participation was instituted.

Second, headteacher leadership also plays an important role (Adu, 2016; Malakolunthu et al., 2014; Yamada, 2014). Headteachers can build and nurture relationships with teachers, parents, and community members (Malakolunthu et al., 2014). The quality of leadership by headteachers has a significant impact on the success or failure of institutionalized school management because they liaise with actors outside of the school (Yamada, 2014). Adu (2016) also stated that school effectiveness and school improvement studies have consistently highlighted the pivotal role of headteachers. The third is those who hold access to outside resources.

This includes actors, such as the SMC or parent–teacher association (PTA) chairperson, who need to approve school improvement plans for the disbursement of government support or proposals to get external assistance (Yamada, 2014).

Though leadership is critical to induce participation, it also hinders participation. The "elite capture" happens when a few educated stakeholders such as headteachers and SMC or PTA chairpersons dominate decision-making in school management while the majority of parents and community members are marginalized (Essuman & Akyeampong, 2011; Pellini, 2005).

Reciprocal and mutual relationships among school-level stakeholders

It is critical to determine how to overcome challenges of conflicts, differentiation, and alienation among school-level stakeholders as the results of institutionalized community participation in school management. Studies have highlighted the significance of the reciprocal relationship between schools and communities (Essuman & Akyeampong, 2011; Pryor, 2005), mutual accountability (Nishimura, 2018), and balance between support and accountability (De Grauwe, 2005). For instance, Essuman and Akyeampong (2011) argued that schools and communities should have the social contract based on the principle of reciprocity and the mutual expectation of execution and accountability of their respective roles. Nishimura (2018) asserted that there is a strong sense of community when people play the roles of both service providers and clients. De Grauwe (2005) articulated that poorly performing schools need support more than they need accountability. In this regard, accountability does not appear to be a one-way process from clients to service providers, but rather it is more collective and mutual, as Nishimura (2018) argued.

Social capital

Social capital is composed of trust, networks, and reciprocal norms and includes reciprocal relationships that are composed of expectations and obligations between two parties (Coleman, 1988). Studies have analyzed social capital from the following aspects: concept, level of analysis, type, and method of measurement.

Regarding the level of analysis, Putnam (2000) describes social capital as connections among individuals – social networks, in which community members trust each other. These connections can be embodied in organizations such as churches, community groups, and families. Coleman (1988) analyzed social capital at the individual level, both in the family and outside the family. Social capital is measured as a family factor (e.g., whether a person has both parents, the number of siblings, and the expectations from their mothers; family bonds; life habits; media control; learning habits; and divorce rate) as well as a community factor (e.g., whether the family has not moved, or whether they enroll children in religiously based private high schools, one's efficacy to live in a community, and rate of house ownership) (Coleman, 1988; Shimizu & Suzuki, 2012; Tsuyuguchi, 2016).

Social capital has been classified into the following modalities: bonding, bridging, and linking social capital (Woolcock, 2001). First, bonding social capital is based on particularized trust and its network is closed and vertical. It exists in church groups, families and friends, and neighborhood associations that share strong connections based on homogeneous interests and backgrounds. Second, bridging social capital is a loose connection among people who have different interests and backgrounds. It is based on general trust and its network is more open and horizontal. It exists in nonprofit organizations and civil society organizations. Lastly, linking social capital is a connection among different individuals and groups with different social backgrounds. It exists in fund mobilization activities, which are conducted by organizations that support socially vulnerable people.

However, several studies have criticized social capital concept because it places emphasis on the traditional values of family structure and equal membership. Tsuyuguchi (2016) mentioned that researchers who accept traditional and conservative recommendations support the concept of social capital, whereas their opponents do not accept it. Selle and Kristin (1999) criticized the fact that Putnam's notion of social capital is based on participatory democracy, in which every member should have face-to-face contacts and opportunities of socialization. They pointed out that democracy should accept both styles of active and passive membership and that one's commitment should not be restricted to face-to-face contacts only but rather should include various modalities. Suetomi (2005) also argued that Putnam's notion of social capital has the assumption of equal membership that parents and community members have affirmative and active preferences to participate in the management of public schools – and that they should pay necessary costs including committing their time. Suetomi (2005) expressed her concerns that parents and community members who are neither affirmative nor active might be marginalized and that this may produce several "free riders" who do not feel obliged to play their roles in schooling.

In developing countries, social capital has been associated with community empowerment and community development. Pryor (2005) argued that community participation discourse assumed that social capital is inherited within the communities surrounding a school; however, the reality is that a community is merely a geographical entity and does not engender a sense of collectiveness. Edwards (2019) argued that community-based management can be thought of as one element of broader efforts to work toward community organization and community building. Essuman (2013) is of the view that there is a reciprocal relationship between schools and geographical communities. Araki (2016) concluded that intrinsic capacity is accumulated and internalized within individuals and communities through various community development activities. They stated that this then becomes an engine and a source of intrinsic motivation for other activities, which resulted in accumulated and synergetic effects.

Research gaps in the literature

A review of available literature reveals that there are several research gaps to be addressed. First, despite accumulated evidence, little has been uncovered as to how community participation affects managerial and pedagogical factors in school management to yield educational outcomes. Bossert (1988) argued that there has been a lack of attention paid to the effects that administrative leadership and school organization have on instruction and student learning. In the conceptual framework of the school effectiveness studies (Schreens, 1990; Heneveld & Craig, 1996), managerial and pedagogical factors in school management appear to have affected each other. However, it is not clear as to how managerial and pedagogical factors should be connected to produce educational outcomes.

Bryk et al. (2010) presented an analytical framework that considers both managerial and pedagogical factors in school management. They identified the linkage between managerial and pedagogical factors and viewed them as the interacting subsystems operating in strong reciprocal causation with one another. However, it is still unknown as to how such reciprocal dynamics occur between the managerial and pedagogical factors in school management.

There appear to be research gaps regarding how the characteristics of effective schools can be applied in the context of developing countries. To this end, it is critical to understand the challenges of school management in developing countries. First, the stability and consistency of school inputs are the most important in developing countries (Fertig, 2000). The teaching profession is regarded as being not financially rewarding owing to its low salary and fringe benefits, especially at the basic education level. This trend results into a high turnover of teachers to other sectors or to higher educational levels (Hedge, 2002). Second, headteachers in developing countries have limited autonomy, an autocratic leadership style, a low degree of initiative to change, and a lack of instructional leadership (Oplatka, 2004). Although there is evidence in developing countries that shows the critical role of headteachers in school improvement (Adu, 2016), it is not possible to assume that the extent of headteacher leadership in developing countries is the same as in developed countries. Finally, some community members and parents do not have the necessary level of literacy and understanding of school needs (Chapman et al., 2002).

De Grauwe (2005) claimed that it is unclear as to the extent to which school-based management has caused higher student achievement through accompanying pedagogical interventions. Edwards (2019) asserted that no studies have examined the actual teaching practices in the case of school-based management intervention in El Salvador. Taniguchi and Hirakawa (2016) argued that in school management, headteachers and teachers were able to enhance student learning achievement, which facilitated community participation.

Second, there is also a research gap regarding how school-level stakeholders have mutual relationships in relation to participation, leadership, and accountability. As described earlier, participation, accountability, and leadership are key terms in community participation in school management (Adu, 2016; Essuman, 2013). However, most studies have emphasized the significance of these terms with a focus on the relationship between participation and accountability (Suzuki, 2002; World Bank, 2003) or between participation and leadership (Essuman & Akyeampong, 2011; Pellini, 2005). Taniguchi and Hirakawa (2016) question how to develop teachers' responsibilities to improve students' achievements and how school leadership and community leadership influence community participation in school management. Therefore, there exists a research gap regarding how leadership, participation, and accountability will work in tandem in role relationships and factors in school management.

As Nishimura (2018) mentioned, mutual accountability occurs as a collaborative effort from a wide range of stakeholders; however, there is no empirical evidence to show how such mutual accountability occurs in the relationships among various school-level stakeholders. There is also no evidence to show how mutual accountability will affect factors in school management and improve educational outcomes, which has been the key theme in school effectiveness studies.

Third, it is critical to know how pupils should be motivated, as they are the subject of learning. Studies into community participation in school management have shown that students are the measurable object of learning in the form of learning outcomes and school enrollment. However, these studies rarely described how students feel and act as the subject of learning. Thus, there still exists a research gap regarding how students will be motivated to learn as the subject of learning, through interactions between school communities, headteachers, teachers, and their guardians.

Relational trust

Characteristics of RT

Bryk and Schneider (2002) classified trust into three categories: organic trust, contractual trust, and RT. First, organic trust concerns the unquestioned beliefs of individuals in the moral authority of a particular social institution. Bryk and Schneider (2002) referred to religious schools, which are part of larger religious communities that embrace a moral vision. However, Bryk and Schneider (2002) argued that the applicability of organic trust breaks down in most modern institutions. Second, they argue that contractual trust is more common in the context of modern institutions. Here, both parties agree with the terms of contract, which spells out the scope of work to be undertaken, or a product or service to be delivered. However, they claim that the social relations around schooling do not fit well within this framework due to the multiple aims of schooling, the complex process of producing student outcomes, and the difficulty in monitoring classroom practices. Finally, they asserted that RT best fits schooling. Its characteristics are mutual dependence among school-level stakeholders. RT is founded both on beliefs and observed behaviors, which make it different from organic and contractual trust. Bryk and Schneider (2002) developed this theory in their study of disadvantaged urban schools with scarce resources under the 1988 Chicago School Reform. They found out that RT affects learning outcomes while also controlling other variables, such as ethnic minorities.

Component of RT: role relationships

Tsuyuguchi (2009) analyzed trust in schools in relation to how parents trust schools using the theory of RT. Bryk and Schneider (2002) considered that RT is the social exchange of schooling as organized around a distinct set of the following role relationships: teachers with pupils; teachers with other teachers; teachers with parents; and teachers with the school principal. They analyzed RT from the viewpoint of teachers. There is a need to analyze these multiple role relationships because this is a critical research gap regarding mitigating conflicts among school-level stakeholders as stipulated in the previous part of this book.

Component of RT: synchronies in mutual expectations and obligations

Bryk and Schneider (2002) asserted that the maintenance and growth of RT in any given set of roles require the synchronies of mutual expectations

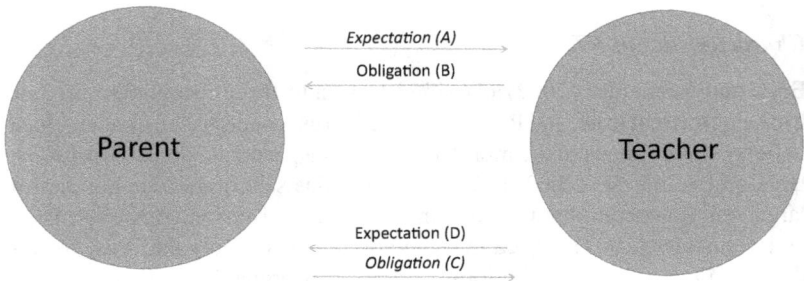

Figure 2.1 Decomposed picture of synchronies in mutual expectations and obliga-
           tions between parent and teacher

Source: Author based on Bryk and Schneider (2002)

and obligations. For instance, as shown in Figure 2.1, parents expect that
teachers will take necessary actions to help their children learn to read (A).
Teachers feel obliged to work in a professionally appropriate manner and
are willing to commit extra effort, if necessary, in seeking to respond to the
parents' expectations (B). Parents, in turn, are obliged to make sure that
their children attend school regularly and more generally to support the
teachers' efforts at home (D). In this case, teachers may expect parents to
perform their duties of rearing their children at home (C). Epstein et al.
(2002) put children at the center of the social relationship among school,
family, and community. In addition, Bryk and Schneider (2002) opined
that RT can make school-level stakeholders go the extra mile for children.
However, it is not evident in the existing literature as to how children are
situated between parents and teachers regarding the exchange of expectations and obligations within RT.

Other studies have adopted the theory of RT in their analytical framework. Tsuyuguchi (2016) articulated that expectations alone cannot be
treated as trust. For instance, those guardians who expect schools to care
about what guardians should do, do not trust but rather depend on schools
when the expectation is highly stressed. Tsuyuguchi (2016) asserted that in
schooling one must have both expectations and obligations to realize RT.
Thus, it is critical to analyze the mutual relationships among the school-
level stakeholders as discussed earlier, from the viewpoint of RT, which has
synchronies in mutual expectations and obligations.

Component of RT: criteria for discernment

Bryk and Schneider (2002) analyzed RT using the criteria for discernment
such as respect, competency, personal regards to others, and integrity in their

qualitative study. Dabney (2008) adopted the concept of RT in a qualitative analysis in terms of the relationship between headteachers and teachers.

Component of RT: reciprocal dynamics between factors in school management

Bryk and Schneider (2002) outlined the relationship between RT and the following core organizational conditions in school management: orientation to innovation, outreach to parents, professional community, and commitment to school communities. Bryk et al. (2010) concluded that there are reciprocal dynamics between RT and the process of school improvement, namely, "Parent, School, Community ties," "School Learning Climate," "Professional Capacity" (managerial factor), and "Classroom Black Box" (pedagogical factor) in school management.

RT and participation

Bryk and Schneider (2002) set the following role relationship for RT: teachers with pupils; teachers with other teachers; teachers with parents; and teachers with the school principal. As described previously, parents/guardians will play their roles in schooling both at collective and individual participation levels. Therefore, I decided to name this collective aspect of the relationship between teachers and parents as "School communities-school RT." This corresponds to collective rust/participation, whereas "Teacher-parent RT" can be categorized as individual trust/participation. "Headteacher-teacher RT" and "Teacher-teacher RT" are also discussed at the collective level as they belong to collectives of teaching professionals.

Research gaps in the literature

There are several research gaps in analyzing RT. First, Bryk and Schneider (2002) quantitatively analyzed RT in each role relationship, based on

Table 2.2 Correspondence between RT and participation

Particularized trust	RT	Participation
Collective trust	School communities–school RT	Collective participation
	Headteacher–teacher RT	
	Teacher–teacher RT	
Individual trust	Teacher–parent RT	Individual participation

Source: Author based on Bryk and Schneider (2002) and Tsuyuguchi (2016)

criteria for discernment. They created a composite indicator of RT to conduct advanced quantitative analysis. On one hand, this has advantages because it can avoid correlations among independent variables when investigating relationships between independent and dependent variables. However, the created composite indicators are unlikely to measure to what extent RT in each role relationship affects the managerial and pedagogical factors in school management, resulting in educational outcomes. Bryk and Schneider (2002) conducted the qualitative analysis with emphasis on the criteria for discernment, such as respect and personal regards, though they mentioned synchronies in expectations and obligations. Moreover, Bryk and Schneider (2002) did not reveal why expectations from one party were met or not met with obligations from the other party.

Tsuyuguchi (2016) articulated that it is necessary for parents not only to expect schools to do something good for their children but also to be obliged to perform their duties for their children. Tsuyuguchi (2003) asserted that because trust is a concept that involves interaction between those who trust and those who are trusted, it is methodologically difficult to gather data from both sides and to identify the extent of trust as the result of interaction. Tsuyuguchi (2016), in this regard, paid attention to parents' trust in schools. In this case, the expectations from parents to school (A) and the obligations from parents to school (C) as shown in Figure 2.1 are ideal for schools that are trusted by parents. With this definition and arrangement, Tsuyuguchi (2016) argued that it is possible to measure the extent of trust or interrelation between parents and school from the perspective of parents.

However, despite these methodological advantages, Tsuyuguchi (2016) did not analyze RT in other role relationships such as between headteacher and teachers, among teachers, and between teachers and parents. In addition, although Tsuyuguchi (2016) suggested that more qualitative analysis is necessary to determine which realities constitute these relationships, few studies in this field have combined both quantitative and qualitative analyses.

In summary, in the context of developing countries, it appears to be important to pay attention to the following components of RT: role relationships; synchronies in mutual expectations and obligations; and reciprocal dynamics among factors in school management. This is because schools in developing countries are confronted with severe resource scarcity, and school-level stakeholders have to depend on each other to support the day-to-day management of schools. Therefore, it would not be adequate to have information as to whether one party has trustworthy characteristics such as criteria for discernment. Instead, it matters whether school-level stakeholders expect headteachers/teachers to perform their duties to educate children, and headteachers/teachers are obliged to perform their duties in return and vice versa. Regarding the arguments presented in school effectiveness/ improvement studies, it is worthwhile to know how such synchronies of mutual expectations and obligations will become reciprocal dynamics among factors in school management, hence I focus on these three components of RT in this study.

References

Adu, S. (2016). *The role of headteacher leadership and community participation in public school improvement in Ghana* [Unpublished doctoral dissertation, University of Sussex].

Ajei, O. M. (2001). *Indigenous knowledge systems and good governance in Ghana: The traditional akan socio-political example* [Occasional dissertations Paper No. 30, Institute of Economic Affairs].

Araki, M. (2016). Intrinsic development practice and creation of commons: Attentions to conflicts and collaboration over water resource management in Tanzania. In M. Takahashi & S. Oyama (Eds.), *Between development and coexistence: Living in the transformation of the nations and the market* (pp. 91–121). Kyoto University Publisher.

Barrera-Osorio, F., Tazeen, F., Patrinos, H. A., & Santibáñez, L. (2009). *Decentralized decision-making in schools: The theory and evidence on school cased management*. World Bank.

Bossert, S. (1988). School effects. In N. Boyan (Ed.), *The handbook of research on educational administration* (pp. 341–354). Longman.

Bray, M. (2000). *Community participation in education: Dimensions, variations, and implications*. The University of Hong Kong, Comparative Education Center.

Bruns, B., Deon, F., & Harry, A. P. (2011). *Making schools work: New evidence on accountability reforms*. World Bank.

Bryk, A. S., & Schneider, B. (2002). *Trust in schools: A core resource for improvement*. Russell Sage Foundation.

Bryk, A. S., Sebring, P. B., Allensworth, E., Luppescu, S., & Easton, J. Q. (2010). *Organizing schools for improvement: Lessons from Chicago*. University of Chicago Press.

Caldwell, B. J. (2005). *School-based management*. UNESCO.

Carolan-Silva, A. (2011). Negotiating the roles of community members and parents: Participation in education in rural paraguay. *Comparative Education Review*, *55*(2), 252–270.

Chapman, C., & Sammons, P. (2013). *School self-evaluation for school improvement: What works and why?* CfBT Education Trust.

Chapman, D., Barcikowski, E., Sowah, M., Gyamera, E., & Woode, G. (2002). Do community know the best? Testing a premise of educational decentralization: Community members' perceptions of their local schools in Ghana. *International Journal of Educational Development*, *22*, 181–189.

Coleman, J. S. (1988). Social capital in the creation of human capital. *American Journal of Sociology*, *94*, 95–120.

Coleman, J. S., Campbell, E. Q., Hobson, C. J., McPartland, J., Mood, A. M., Weinfeld, F. D., & York, R. L. (1966). *Equality of educational opportunity.* U.S. Department of Health, Education, and Welfare, Office of Education.

Cuellar-Marchelli, H. (2003). Decentralization and privatization of education in El Salvador: Assessing the experience. *International Journal of Educational Development, 23,* 145–166.

Dabney, J. (2008). *Show me that you care: The presence of relational trust between a principal and teachers in an urban school* [Unpublished doctoral dissertation, Ohio State University].

De Grauwe, A. (2005). Improving the quality of education through school based management: Learning from international experiences. *International Review of Education, 51*(4), 269–287.

Edwards Jr., D. B. (2019). Shifting the perspective on community-based management of education: From systems theory to social capital and community empowerment. *International Journal of Educational Development, 64,* 17–26.

Edwards Jr., D. B., & Klees, S. J. (2015). Unpacking 'participation' in development and educational governance: A framework of perspectives and practices. *Prospects, 45,* 483–499.

Epstein, J. L., Sanders, M. G., Simon, B. S., Salinas, K. C., Jansorn, N. R., & Van Voorhis, F. L. (2002). *School, family, and community partnerships: Your handbook for action* (2nd ed.). Corwin Press Inc., A Sage Publications Company.

Essuman, A. (2013). *Decentralization of education management in Ghana: Key issues in school-community relations.* LAP LAMBERT Academic Publishing.

Essuman, A., & Akyeampong, K. (2011). Decentralisation policy and practice in Ghana: The promise and reality of community participation in education in rural community. *Journal of Education Policy, 26*(4), 513–527.

Fertig, M. (2000). Old wine in new bottles? Researching effective schools in developing countries. *School Effectiveness and School Improvement, 11*(3), 385–403.

Gershberg, A. I., Gonzalez, P. A., & Meade, B. (2012). Understanding and improving accountability in education: A conceptual framework and guideposts from three decentralization reform experiences in Latin America. *World Development, 40*(5), 1024–1041.

Hedge, J. (2002). The importance of posting and interaction with the education bureaucracy in becoming a teacher in Ghana. *International Journal of Educational Development, 22,* 353–366.

Heneveld, W., & Craig, H. (1996). *School counts.* World Bank Project Designs and the Quality of Primary Education in Sub-Saharan Africa. World Bank.

Hoppers, W. (2005). Community schools as an educational alternative in Africa: A critique. *International Review of Education, 51*(2–3), 115–137.

Lockheed, M. E., & Levin, H. M. (1993). Creating effective schools. In H. M. Levin & M. E. Lockheed (Eds.), *Effective schools in developing countries.* The Falmer Press.

Lockheed, M. E., & Verspoor, A. (1991). *Improving primary education in developing countries.* World Bank.

Malakolunthu, S., McBeath, J., & Swaffield, S. (2014). Improving the quality of teaching and learning through leadership for learning: Changing scenarios in basic schools of Ghana. *Educational Management Administration and Leadership*, *42*(5), 701–717.

Martiniello, M. (2000). Participacion de los Padres en la Educacion: Hacia una Taxonomia para America Latina. In J. C. Navarro, K. Taylor, & A. Bernasconi (Eds.), *Perspectivas sobre la reforma educativa: America central en el contexto de politicas de educacion en Las America*. United States Agency for International Development.

Mfum-Mensah, O., & Friedson-Ridenour, S. (2014). Whose voices are being heard? Mechanism for community participation in education in Northern Ghana. *Prospects*, *44*, 351–365.

Mitchell, R. (2017). *An ethnographic case study of the agendas, participation and influence of stakeholders at an urban government primary school in Tigray, Ethiopia* [Unpublished PhD dissertation, University of Leicester].

Nishimura, M. (2017). Community participation in school management in developing countries. *Oxford Research Encyclopedia of Education*. https://doi.org/10.1093/acrefore/9780190264093.013.64

Nishimura, M. (2018). Community participation in school governance: The Massai community in Kenya. *Prospects*. https://doi.org/10.1007/s11125-018-9439-8

Nyamnjoh, F. B. (2016). Incompleteness: Frontier Africa and the currency of conviviality (K. Kusunoki & M. Matsuda, Trans.). In M. Matsuda & M. Hirano-Nomoto (Eds.), *Cultural creativity for conflict resolution and coexistence: African potentials as practice of incompleteness and bricolage* (pp. 311–347). Kyoto University Press.

Ogawa, M. (2017). Various conflicts emerging in the process of quality improvement in secondary schools in Western Kenya: Decisions by schools and students. *Comparative Education*, *54*, 88–109.

Okitsu, T., & Edwards Jr, B. D. (2017). Policy promise and the reality of community involvement in school-based management in Zambia: Can the rural poor hold schools and teachers to account? *International Journal of Educational Development*, *56*, 28–41.

Oplatka, I. (2004). The principalship in developing countries: Context, characteristics and reality. *Comparative Education*, *40*(3), 427–448.

Pellini, A. (2005). Decentralization of education in Cambodia: Searching for spaces of participation between traditions and modernity. *Compare*, *35*(2), 205–216.

Pryor, J. (2005). Can community participation mobilize social capital for improvement of rural schooling? A case study from Ghana. *Compare*, *35*(2), 193–203.

Putnam, R. D. (2000). *Bowing alone: The collapse and revival of American community*. Simon & Schuster.

Rose, P. (2003). Community participation in school policy and practice in Malawi: Balancing local knowledge, national policies and international agency priorities. *Compare*, *33*(1), 47–64. https://doi.org/10.1080/03057920302597

Saito, K. (2013). Community participation in school management in Senegal: Differences between behavior and perception. *Comparative Education*, *46*, 80–101.

Sammons, P., Hillman, J., & Mortimore, P. (1995). *Key characteristics of effective schools: A review of school effectiveness research*. London: OFSTED.

Sanders, M. G. (2002). Community involvement in school improvement: The little extra that makes a big difference. In J. L. Epstein, M. G. Sanders, B. S. Simon, K. C. Salinas, N. R. Jansorn, & F. L. Van Voorhis (Eds.), *School, family, and community partnerships: Your handbook for action* (2nd ed.). Corwin Press Inc., A Sage Publications Company.

Schreens, J. (1990). School effectiveness research and the development of process indicators of school functioning. *School Effectiveness and School Improvement, 12*, 61–80.

Selle, P., & Kristin, S. (1999). Organizational membership and democracy: Do we need to consider passive members seriously? (Ogawa, A). University of Chiba. *Journal of Law and Politics, 14*(1), 143–166.

Sergiovanni, T. (1994). *Building community in schools.* Jossey-Bass Publishers.

Shimizu, K., & Suzuki, I. (2012). *Comparative sociology of learning improvement policies: What did the national learning survey bring to prefectures?* Akashi Publishers.

Stoll, L. (1996). Linking school effectiveness and school improvement: Issues and possibilities. In J. Gray (Ed.), *Merging traditions: Future of research on school effectiveness and school improvement* (pp. 30–50). Continuum International Publishing Group Ltd.

Suetomi, K. (2005). Public schools as club goods and their membership issues: Position of passive members in decentralized education reforms. *Japan Educational Administration Society Bulletin, 31*, 133–150.

Suzuki, I. (2002). Parental participation and accountability in primary schools in Uganda. *Compare, 32*(2), 243–259.

Takeda, N., Demas, A., & Shibuya, K. (2013). *World Bank portfolio review of school autonomy and accountability: Operations and analytical work FY 2003–2013.* World Bank.

Taniguchi, K., & Hirakawa, Y. (2016). Dynamics of community participation, student achievement and school management: The case of primary schools in a rural area of Malawi. *Compare, 46*(3), 479–502.

Tsuyuguchi, K. (2003). Headteacher leadership seeking for trust building: Relationship between leadership, trust, and school improvement. *Research Bulletin of Educational Administration, 6*, 21–37.

Tsuyuguchi, K. (2009). The relationship between the organization image which parents have and the school trust: An analysis which utilized individual and organizational level data. *Bulletin of the Faculty of Education, Ehime University, 56*, 27–36.

Tsuyuguchi, K. (Ed.). (2016). *Social capital and education: Role of school in creating connections.* Minerva Publishing Company.

Welsh, T., & McGinn, N. F. (1999). *Decentralization of education: Why, when, what and how?.* UNESCO/IIEP.

Woolcock, M. (2001). The place of social capital in understanding social and economic outcomes. In J. F. Helliwall (Ed.), *The contribution of human and social capital to sustained growth and well-being: International symposium report.* Human Resourced Development Canada and OECD.

World Bank. (2003). *World development report 2004.* World Bank and Oxford University Press.

World Bank. (2013). *Project appraisal document for quality improvement and equity of basic education project.* World Bank.

Yamada, S. (2014). Determinants of 'community participation': The tradition of local initiatives and the institutionalization of school management committees in Oromia Region, Ethiopia. *Compare, 44*(2), 162–185.

Yntiso, G., Ohta, I., & Matsuda, M. (2017). Introduction: Achieving peace and coexistence through African potentials. In G. Yntiso, I. Ohta, & M. Matsuda (Eds.), *African virtues in the pursuit of conviviality: Exploring local solutions in light of global prescriptions* (pp. 3–37). Langaa, Bwea.

Yu, G. (2007). *Research evidence of school effectiveness in Sub-Saharan Africa.* EdQUAL Working Paper No. 7. University of Bristol.

3 Community participation in school management in Ghana

Introduction

This chapter introduces to the readers the education system, the historical background of schooling, and the status of educational outcomes in terms of access, quality, and pupil discipline in order to understand the educational context in Ghana. Access to basic education has been improved significantly in Ghana. School communities pay special attention to the pupils' achievements, the BECE, which determines pupils' progression to senior high schools. On the other, pupils' discipline has become an acute challenge owing to poor parenting, extended family system, and youth employment. The literature review describes indigenous geographical communities, cultural communities, and school communities in Ghana. In view of this, the SMCs have been established as an institutionalized form of participation in school management. This chapter also describes how teachers and head-teachers are positioned and regarded in the education system and how local and educational administration support school management.

Schooling system, its historical background, and educational outcomes in Ghana

In this section, I describe the following educational context in Ghana: schooling system; the historical background of establishing schools; the status of educational outcomes from the perspectives of access (enrollment), quality (learning achievement), and pupils' discipline.

Schooling system

The schooling system in Ghana has the following cycle: preschool-KG (2 years), primary school (6 years), JHS (3 years), senior high school (SHS) (3 years), and higher education (Polytechnic, College of Education, and

DOI: 10.4324/9781003320579-3

University) (3–4 years). Compulsory education covers KG, primary school, and JHS where all parents are obligated to send their children to school. Some basic schools have all the three levels of education – KG, primary school, and JHS, while others stand alone as KG, KG and primary, and JHS. Pupils who graduate from basic schools without a JHS section must look for a convenient JHS to complete their basic education and then who want to proceed can enter the SHS based on their performance at the BECE.

Historical background of establishing public schools

In Ghana, generally speaking, geographical communities expect local education administration to establish public primary schools. However, some geographical communities for any reason could put up structures to start a school, and later the schools are absorbed by the local education administration after satisfying all requirements for the establishment of a school. Having satisfied with the requirements, the local education administration deploys qualified teachers to the schools to teach and then register them as public schools. As most of these geographical communities may not have the resources, they are not able to build all the necessary structures; thus, some schools may start without enough classrooms from KG one to Primary six and also without school canteens, urinals and toilets, staff rooms, or storeroom. In the case that they have fewer classrooms than the enrollment for all the grade levels, the schools adopt the multigrade teaching where more than one grade level of pupils are combined in one classroom and taught by one or more teachers. If primary schools have enough pupils to proceed to the JHS, the geographical communities may request the Ghana Education Service (GES) headquarters through the district education office to establish JHSs to be attached to these primary schools. The GES headquarters will appraise the request and when satisfied by the conditions, approval shall be granted, and the JHS established. The local education administration then deploys teachers to the JHS and provides the necessary facilities and materials to enable the school to function. The District Assembly (DA) has an annual budget for constructing or renovating schools in the district; however, in most cases, the budget can only cover a few schools per year, hence the initiatives of the geographical communities in the establishment of basic schools are essential.

Access to basic education

Access to basic education in Ghana has made remarkable progress in recent decades. In 2020, the net enrollment rates at primary and lower secondary level schools were, respectively, 82.4% and 62%, while the gross enrollment rates were, respectively, 103.44% and 77.67% (UNESCO Institute of

Statistics, n.d.). According to Darvas and Balwanz (2014), in 2008/2009, the average enrollment in per KG, primary school, and JHS were, respectively, 90, 225 and 138, respectively. However, the medium of school enrollment in per KG, primary school, and JHS was 80, 193, and 112, respectively. This means that school enrollment per school is lower than the average. Thus, as Darvas and Balwanz (2014) argued, primary education in Ghana is largely delivered by small and medium schools.

In Ghana, guardians are not necessarily supposed to enroll their children in schools that are located within the geographical boundaries they reside. Thus, in practice, guardians can choose any KG, primary school, or JHS for their children provided that there are vacancies in the said schools, and if guardians have the needed financial means to support their children's education regarding transportation and other costs not borne by the government. They may choose private schools if they can afford to pay fees. Thus, school enrollment is an important indicator for school management of public basic schools owing to the following reasons. First, it tells the scale of a school, including school infrastructure, which also dictates the preference of a school and also represents the reputation of the guardian. If guardians perceive that a school has desirable learning achievements or provides a conducive learning environment, they will send their children to such schools. Second, as school enrollment increases, the government budget for such schools also increases. The government capitation grant to schools is calculated per student and consequently per school enrollment, and the higher the enrollment, the bigger the quantum of capitation grant to be received by the school. In addition, the higher the enrollment, the higher the total dues to be mobilized by the PTA to support the schools' infrastructure development. Third, for basic schools without a JHS section, school enrollment in the primary section is an important indicator that shows the necessity for a JHS. As such, school enrollment is significant for school management.

Quality of education from the perspective of the BECE

The BECE is a national standardized examination held every year (at the end of basic education) for JHS Grade 3 students, who must take the examination to complete their basic education cycle and proceed to SHSs. Seventy percent of a student's total score comes from the BECE results, while 30% is from the continuous assessment results. The results of six subjects are made up of four core subjects (mathematics, science, English, and social studies) and two other subjects that are computed to get the overall score for each candidate of the BECE. Each subject is scored at 100 points and the aggregate score of each subject will be assigned to each candidate from one (best) to nine (worst) based on the distribution of scores among the candidates that took part in the examination. To determine their admissions to a SHS, a student's mean aggregate for the six subjects is utilized, and the smaller mean aggregate represents the better performance. The minimum admission qualification for a SHS is to obtain an aggregate score below six for the core subjects. Guardians and community members pay special attention to the BECE results as it determines whether a student can proceed to a SHS or not. The BECE mean aggregate at each school is an important indicator because students with the highest aggregate score (1–6) have greater opportunities to be enrolled in top-performing SHSs of their choice.

Pupils' discipline as an emerging concern

Unlike access to and quality of education, pupils' discipline has rarely been discussed in the education sector development plans of developing countries, including Ghana. However, pupils' discipline is the highest concern for parents and teachers. Pupils' discipline has become an emerging concern for Ghanaian society, which compelled me to include it as part of the educational outcomes in this study. I refer to the following factors that could affect pupils' discipline: youth employment, extended family system, poor parenting, and corporal punishment.

Youth (JHS graduates) employment

As shown in the net and gross enrollment at primary and JHS levels, access to basic education has been expanded rapidly in Ghana. However, the gaps between the net and the gross enrollment rates show that there are pupils who are "over age" beyond appropriate school-age level and who are currently enrolled in schools. Studies show that some community members do not value the skills being taught in schools because they do not see those skills necessarily to contribute to their economic wealth. Thus, youth in especially poor communities are likely to be engaged in youth employment in order to earn money to support themselves and their families. "Okada" drivers who transport passengers on motorbikes without licenses is one example (Sefa-Nyarko et al., 2018). This can lead to youths or overaged pupils dropping out of school to take up such menial jobs or would be working after school to earn money (Volta Online, 2018). Under this context, these students are unlikely to be committed to learning and do not put a value on education.

Extended family system

In Ghana, it has been a common practice for seasonal migrants to leave their children in the daily care of grandparents and/or relatives. The 2010 Population and Housing Census showed that single-parent families (nuclear, extended, extended +non relatives) owing to death, divorce, or working outside of geographical boundaries occupy 24.7% of the national house-hold population. Andrews (2017) posited that an extended family system links with poverty and affects one's capacity to be fully involved in a child's education. Essuman (2013) also asserted that many children are being fos-tered by relatives other than their biological parents and that grandparents and distant relatives may not have the same degree of commitment and knowledge of the child's welfare in schools and may therefore participate less in school affairs.

Poor parenting

Sefa-Nyarko et al. (2018) expressed the view that "poor parenting" is a hindering factor that influences low secondary school completion rate. Poor parenting includes a lack of support and supervision of the student. Such support may be financial, including the provision of food, textbooks, writ-ing materials, and/or payment of PTA fees, while non-financial includes encouraging students to stay in school, encouraging dropout students to return to school, or participating in school activities such as PTA meetings. Supervision may also include monitoring children's attendance in school to avoid truancy, checking whether homework had been done or not and ensuring that children are at home instead of wasting their time at night-clubs or funerals (Sefa-Nyarko et al., 2018). Studies have also shown that most parents believe that they do not have the resources and tools to educate their children, and that is why they overly rely on teachers to provide the required support for their children's education (Ampadu et al., 2017).

Corporal punishment

It has been a common practice in Africa for teachers to use cane to disci-pline pupils when they go wrong or misbehave (Alhassan, 2013). There have been several attempts to prevent teachers from using cane; however, it currently prevails as common practices in Ghana (Andrews, 2017). In 2017, the GES issued a directive to ban any form of corporal punishment, including the use of cane. This provoked controversial and dichotomous discussions among school-level stakeholders as to whether they should or should not use canes to discipline children. While some argue that caning is a form of assault, some assert that a ban on caning will break down pupil discipline in schools (Afanyi-Dadzie, 2019; Lartey, 2019; Nyanbor, 2019). Andrews (2017) argued that corporal punishment contributes to discourag-ing parents from participating in education; however, he also admitted that there are dichotomies in opinions between parents and teachers in terms of the use of corporal punishment in Ghana.

Indigenous geographical communities' participation in school management

Ghana has a traditional chieftaincy system across the country ranging from a local-level chief to a paramountcy-level chief or king where such paramount chiefs have jurisdiction over the local-level chiefs (Hirose, 2011). The traditional chiefs and elders meet often to discuss issues affecting the locality and take decisions to address them, for example, educational issues such as indiscipline in schools or poor infrastructure. Participation of community members and consensus building of ideas form a major component of the local-level decision-making process by the traditional authorities (Ajei, 2001). Currently, local government or local education administration is responsible for constructing and renovating schools and deploying teachers to the local schools. However, traditional chiefs or authorities still appear to be influential in deciding on issues affecting the schools, for example, the need for the deployment of teachers to the local schools by the local education authorities due to the strong leadership and charisma of the chiefs (Hirose, 2011).

Actors, except for the government, have been involved in establishing schools since the British colonial era of the Gold Coast in the 1920s (Foster, 1965; McWilliam, 1957). Records from the colonial government's administration at the beginning of the 20th century show that local elites and traditional chiefs had been actively engaged in constructing and establishing schools (Yamada, 2011). Traditional chiefs, missionaries, and local elites in collaboration with geographical communities supported schools with provision of labor and money and sometimes hired teachers for schools. As these schools developed with community initiatives, the management and control of the schools thus shifted to central government authorities, and communities tended to become less actively involved (Adam, 2005; Essuman, 2013). Essuman (2013) argued that international literature on education decentralization often does not place as much empirical interests in indigenous geographical communities in contributing to the development of schools as it does with the officially designated groups such as SMCs or PTAs.

Cultural community

Among the types of community described earlier, cultural communities in Ghana are diverse in terms of religion, ethnicity, language, gender, and generations. According to the Ministry of Foreign Affairs in Japan, Ghana has several religions (about 70% are Christians, and 17% being Muslims), along with other indigenous religions and over 80 ethnic groups (Yamada, 2011). When geographical communities are divided into different cultural, ethnic, or linguistic groups, school communities need rigorous coordination over the use of language of instruction, the kind of school events to undertake, and membership of the school management body (Nishimura, 2017). Pryor (2005) argued that a geographical community does not engender a sense of collectiveness because there are disruptions to these communities from migration and the disintegration of matrilineal family structures, which affect the dispositions of rural people to schooling.

Institutionalized school communities' participation in school management

Universal primary education policies

The Government of Ghana embarked on two major educational reforms in 1987 and 1996. In the 1987 reform, the role of the local community to participate in basic education collectively and collaboratively was emphasized to improve access to education (Essuman, 2013). In 1996, the free, compulsory, universal basic education (fCUBE) program was introduced, based on the 1992 Constitution of Ghana, which required the government to provide quality basic education for all Ghanaian children, irrespective of race, gender, religion, location, or tribe (Adu, 2016). The objectives included (1) improving access and participation in education (ensuring that all the school-going children are in school and complete basic education), (2) improving the quality of teaching and learning (promoting efficient and effective quality teaching and learning), and (3) improving efficiency in management (securing efficiency, probity, and accountability in the management of schools).

Policies and practices in decentralization, deconcentration, and community participation in school management

In Ghana, decentralization reforms have accelerated to shift the responsibilities of the central government to local government, referred to as the DA in Ghana. In 1988, by the Local Government Law, 10 regions and 110 districts were created in Ghana, and the DA, which is politically headed by the District Chief Executive, became the unit of decentralization. In the education sector, currently, DAs have the budget for school construction and infrastructure repair. The Education Act 778 also provided for a decentralized pre-tertiary education system, which was aimed to strengthen the role of DAs in the provision of educational administration, which is currently at the premise of the GES district education office.

In 1995, the Parliament enacted the GES Act (Act 506), which promoted the decentralization policies in education. The GES headquarters was responsible for educational administration at the national level, whereas regional directors of education and district directors of education were responsible for the provincial and district levels, respectively. The 1995 GES Act also established the SMC. SMCs are under the supervision of the Municipal/District Education Oversight Committee, to which the Municipal/District Chief Executive belongs.

Policies and practices of community participation in school management have been emphasized over the years in Ghana. To supplement the school fee abolishment policies, the government introduced the capitation grant (CG) scheme in 2005, starting with Three Ghana Cedis (GHC3.00) three per pupil per year (Note: GHC 1.00 was equivalent to USD 0.18 as of October 20, 2019). From 2009, it increased to GHC 4.50. Subsequently, the school report card (SRC) was introduced to report on the performance of schools and pupils' achievements to parents/guardians. The School Performance Appraisal Meeting (SPAM) was also launched as an avenue to discuss school performance and the necessary measures taken to address any challenges as an accountability system at the school level.

The following interventions have been implemented with support from development partners in Ghana: the Whole School Development (WSD) funded by the UK Department for International Development, the Quality Improvement Primary School project funded by the United States Agency for International Development, the Ghana Partnership for Education Project funded by Global Partnership for Education, the E-School Report Card project implemented by United Nations Children's Funds, and other projects implemented by various nongovernment organizations (NGOs) (Akyeampong, 2004).

Among these interventions, the WSD program was a holistic intervention run under the fCUBE program. It featured the following components: child-centered primary practices in literacy, numeracy and problem-solving; community participation in education delivery; provision of support to headteachers and teachers; participatory planning and resource management at school and district levels; and improvement of efficiency in resource management (Akyeampong, 2004). Akyeampong (2004) explained some teething problems for the WSD. For instance, SMCs expected greater transparency and accountability from headteachers, which may have been considered as being intrusive by headteachers and teachers. Other problems are that no or limited resources have been provided to schools, and headteachers have also experienced difficulties in motivating teachers in the absence of rewards and incentives.

School management committees and parent teacher associations

Both SMCs and PTAs have similar objectives but have different characteristics in terms of their objectives, membership, meetings, and source of funding.

The SMC is mandated to engage in the following activities (p. 15) (Ghana Education Service, 2012):

- Participate in establishing priorities and setting goals and developing strategies for school improvement
- Regularly encourage parents and other community members to participate in school's improvement planning and implementation processes
- Review schools' progress in implementing the SPIP with their headteachers
- Support the development of team and leadership skills for both teachers and learners in schools
- Implement mechanisms to hold headteachers and staff accountable for progress toward the goals set out in the SPIP
- Contribute to the development of the SPIP

SMC executive members are composed of the following (p. 19) (Ghana Education Service, 2012):

- District Director of Education or representative
- DA representative (assembly members)
- Unit committee (administrative units under the DA) representative
- Chief's representative
- PTA representative
- Headteacher
- Two members of the teaching staff
- Co-opted members to perform specific functions (optional)

There are three types of SMC meeting: general meetings (in which all the members of the SMC attend), executive meetings (in which elected executive members attend), and emergency meetings. While it has been suggested that the SPIP should be developed in consultation with the whole school communities, it is not clear in the handbook as to whether all community members will be invited to the general meetings to discuss the SPIP. The District Chief Executive chairs the District Education Oversight Committee, which implies that the SMC is a school-level unit of decentralized education system. The sources of funding of SMCs include the PTA funds raised through contributions by parents and donations from NGOs, corporate bodies, and individuals. SMCs do not have their own means of income generation.

GES has been collecting the following information from the Education Management Information System (EMIS) data every year: the existence of elected SMCs and the frequency of the meetings; the existence of a SPIP; and the receipt of the CG (for the previous year).

On the other hand, PTAs have the following objectives and memberships (p. 29) (Ghana Education Service, 2012):

- To promote the welfare of children and youths at home, at school, and in the community, through a strong linkage
- To assist in income generating activities to provide some basic needs for the school
- To raise the standards of children at home
- To secure adequate by-laws for the care and protection of children
- To bring into closer relation the home and the school, so that parents and teachers may cooperate intelligently regarding the education of their children
- To develop between educators and the general public such united efforts that will secure for all children the highest advantages in physical, mental, social, and spiritual education.

PTAs comprise the parents and guardians who have their children together with the teachers in that particular school. The source of funding is mainly voluntary financial contributions from parents in the form of PTA dues. In terms of meetings, there are both PTA executive and general meetings, but there is no specific explanation about these meetings in the handbook (Ghana Education Service, 2012).

Adu (2016) stated that the PTAs are more active than SMCs because PTA can generate their own funds to service their meetings by providing snacks to members who attend, whereas SMCs do not have any funds as such unless supported by the PTAs. Essuman (2013) described the contrast between SMCs and PTAs in terms of attitude and methods of involvement in school activities. PTA members generally appear to be more supportive and collaborative and pay more attention to pupils than to teachers, whereas SMC members function as inspectors of schools. Thus, although they are expected to work in tandem to improve schools (Ghana Education Service, 2012), SMCs and PTAs appear to have different features and focus. Darvas and Balwanz (2014) argued that the degree of support for PTAs is strongly linked to their level of income. For instance, financial support for PTAs in schools located within wealthier areas is on average tenfold more than schools in the poorest areas.

Challenges in institutionalized community participation

Studies in Ghana have identified the following challenges in institutionalized community participation in Ghana: the community members' low SES (value on education, and income), the lack of will for participation, the knowledge and capacity of community members to manage schools (Mfum-Mensah & Friedson-Ridenour, 2014; Donkor, 2010), and the conflicts between teachers and parents, due to the fear of teachers that parents will invade teachers' professional autonomy (Essuman & Akyeampong, 2011).

In the literature, Adu (2016) and Essuman (2013) attempted to reveal the relationships between community and schools, or among teachers, head-teachers, and parents/community members, through qualitative research. Adu (2016) analyzed two high-performing schools, identifying the actors (teachers, headteachers, and parents and community members) and the factors for school improvement. Adu found that teacher commitment to curriculum change, headteacher leadership, and parent/community participation are keys to successful school management.

However, there are several research gaps in his study. First, in the analytical framework of the conclusion, Adu (2016) did not adequately show the means by which the two-way relationships function between teacher commitment and curriculum change and between headteachers' leadership and parent/community participation. Second, though the factors for school improvement were described in detail, the study did not show how these factors were related in a way that would lead to school improvement. Finally, although the relationships between headteachers and teachers and between headteachers and parents/community members were described, Adu (2016) did not mention how teachers and parents work together to improve the situation of schools or pupils.

Essuman (2013) conducted case studies of two schools and conceptualized community–school relations by paying attention to capacity, leadership, and accountability. He revealed that it is necessary for school communities such as PTAs, SMCs, and school management to collaborate more with wider geographical communities. However, there are the following research gaps to be addressed. First, Essuman (2013) analyzed how accountability and leadership matter to community participation; however, the study did not reveal how community–school relations will affect educational outcomes. Second, Essuman (2013) highlighted the significance of reciprocity between communities and schools but did not clearly identify how to measure such reciprocity. Lastly, the study did not uncover how such reciprocity occurs in the factors that affect educational outcomes.

Teachers, headteachers, and local government/ educational administration

Teachers

Ghana has the following categories of teachers: qualified teachers employed by GES directly from colleges of education and unqualified teachers employed under certain conditions through government initiatives, such as the national service scheme or national youth employment program, on short-term basis, or hired by the community as community assistant teachers. As shown in Table 3.1, the higher the education level, the higher the percentage of qualified teachers. There are different educational qualifications among these qualified teachers. To be qualified to teach at basic schools, one must obtain a diploma in basic education or certificate A teacher. To teach at a SHS, a bachelor's degree or higher degree (master's) is required.

Shortage of teachers has been an acute problem in rural areas. When teachers are posted to rural areas, many teachers try to get an immediate transfer because of the conditions there, which they find to be unfavorable. Female teachers, who make up over 30% of training college graduates, are usually not posted to rural areas because many parents are opposed to it (Hedge, 2002). Study leave scheme also leads to teacher shortage, where for instance every year, there are approximately 4,000 teachers from the basic school on study leave, while 6,000 students graduate from teacher training colleges (Hedge, 2002).

The low status and motivation of teachers have affected teachers' career paths. Akyeampong and Stephens (2002) interviewed 400 student teachers to discern their expectations and aspirations to become teachers. They concluded that teachers in Ghana face some challenges, including working in deprived areas confronted with dangerous diseases; problems with communication due to language differences between teachers and community; problems with decent accommodation in rural communities; conflicts with community members and parents because of pupils' poor academic performance; and lack of interest of rural communities in education and unnecessary scrutiny of teachers' lifestyle in the rural communities. They argued that these challenges as mentioned have important implications for teachers' long-term commitments in Ghana.

In Ghana, the salary structure for teachers depends on their job title/description as GES staff. If teachers graduate from universities, they will start with "Principal Superintendent Professional," which is a higher rank than "Senior Superintendent II Professional" (those who graduated from a college of education). Teachers become eligible for study leave after 3 years of teaching.

Table 3.1 Number of teachers and qualified teachers in public basic and secondary schools in 2017/2018 academic year

	Number of teachers (A)	Number of qualified teachers (B)	Percentage (B/A)
Kindergarten	42,666	32,084	75.2%
Primary	109,220	91,477	83.8%
JHS	90,818	83,090	91.5%
SHS	40,341	37,048	91.8%

Source: EMIS

Hedge (2002) noted that GES officials regarded the teaching professions, especially at the basic education level, as a "stepping-stone" to a higher job career. Akyeampong and Stephens (2002) also highlighted the low status of teachers, especially in primary schools, that compels them to seek for better status outside teaching or even within teaching but at a higher level of education. Thus, for the sake of their own social mobility, teachers tend to pursue their individual careers rather than serving the community where schools are located. With such a situation, unless geographical communities show that they value the contribution of the teachers to their children's education by providing them with some benefits such as the provision of foodstuff and accommodation, teachers may not accept their services in such communities (Hedge, 2002).

The low social status of teachers also affects teacher accountability. Essuman (2013) argued that community members were concerned with teacher absenteeism to a large extent and monitored their attendance in schools. One of the reasons why teachers may be absent or late to school is that they live in towns that are not in the geographical communities close to their schools. The lack of public transportation sometimes prevents teachers from coming to school on time, as expected. In addition to delays in salary payment, teachers also have difficulties in paying for transportation costs, which eventually affect teacher accountability.

Headteachers

"Principal Superintendent Head Basic" is the minimum requirement to qualify to become headteacher of a basic school. The District Director of Education, Akatsi South District, showed the following promotion process of headteachers. First, vacancies for headteachers are identified resulting from headteachers going on transfer, retirement, or for other reasons. Second, a call for applications to fill the headteachers' vacancy is publicized or notified through the district education office. The qualified applicants will be invited to attend an interview with a panel of interviewees set up at the district education office. Those who are successful, based on the vacancies declared, are officially appointed and promoted to become basic school headteachers. There is a responsibility allowance for basic school headteachers (the amount depends on an approved percentage of the person's basic salary) in addition to the person's basic salary structure. Headteachers can become a member of conference of heads of basic schools (COHBS), which handles the welfare of headteachers including retirement benefits.

The role of headteachers at the basic education level is stipulated in the *Headteacher's Handbook* as follows (Ghana Education Service, 2010):

• Manage people (setting up school committees, delegating duties to school staff, maintaining discipline in school, holding staff meetings, keeping records and filing documents, and maintaining good interpersonal relationships and a code of professional conduct)

- Manage instructional time (orientation to syllabuses, teaching and learning materials, writing lesson plans, planning school timetable, and ensuring compliance to the instructional time)
- Manage cocurricular activities (sports, excursions, and others)
- Manage teaching and learning resources (school buildings; major maintenance; school compound; furniture; stationery; school library; equipment and tools; receiving, distributing, and storing supplies; and stock taking)
- Manage school finance (school funds, CG, and school accounts)
- Improve quality of learning (SPIP, SRC, and SPAMs)
- Increase school intake and attendance (increasing enrollment, preventing dropouts and absenteeism, and identifying children who drop out)
- Assess pupil performance including school-based assessment
- Assess teacher performance
- Staff development including in-service training
- Improve relationships between school and community (PTAs, religious organizations, and SMCs)

In summary, the roles of headteachers are multiple and wide, and the scope is increasing as it plays a pivotal role to manage teachers, community, parents, and local education administrators.

Many studies in Ghana have shown that the status of headteachers at the basic education level in Ghana is not attractive. Hedge (2002) argued that none of the teachers interviewed wanted to become heads of primary schools. The GES officials whom I interviewed during the field study indicated that the reasons why headteacher's position at the basic education level in Ghana is not so attractive are associated with the following teachers' motivations. First, some teachers ranked "Principal Superintendent" or above would like to work in urban schools as teachers at the primary or secondary level, or as assistant headteachers, to avoid being posted as headteachers in rural areas. This is because they and their families prefer the convenient lifestyle in urban areas unlike in rural areas. Furthermore, a headteacher's job at the basic education level is tedious and not financially rewarding and cannot attract fringe benefits as teachers in the senior high schools or tutors in the Colleges of Education.

Local government and educational administration

According to Darvas and Balwanz (2014), while the GES Act (1995) deconcentrated management functions from the central to the district level, the Education Act (2008) devolved decision-making and financing authority to the Metropolitan, Municipal, and District Assemblies. This parallel system of deconcentrated and decentralized lines appears to be complex at the field level.

Darvas and Balwanz (2014) explain that the GES is responsible for the personnel emolument, the supplies, and the disbursement of the CG. The

DA has the budget of the District Assembly Common Funds and is also responsible in seeing to the infrastructure development of the Ghana Education Trust Fund (GETFund). The DA is also responsible for monitoring the Ghana School Feeding Program, which is funded by the Ministry of Local Government and Rural Development.

The GES district education offices have the following several units: administration, finance, logistics, and inspection. Circuit supervisors (CS) belong to the inspection unit, and they inspect a group of schools clustered by circuits. The CS perform the following duties: to provide information from the district to the schools and from the schools to the district offices; to visit schools and monitor teacher and pupil attendance; to check teachers' lesson notes and lesson delivery; and inspect school facilities. They usually attend SMC or PTA executive and general meetings on behalf of the District Director of Education, as stipulated in the SMC Resource Handbook. They vet the SPIP when it was submitted to the district education offices. They are also engaged in distributing the Education Management Information System (EMIS) questionnaire to schools and collecting it from schools to the district office.

References

Adam, F. (2005). *Community participation in school development: Understanding participation in basic schools performance in the Nanumba district of Ghana* [Unpublished master thesis, University of Sussex].

Adu, S. (2016). *The role of headteacher leadership and community participation in public school improvement in Ghana* [Unpublished doctoral dissertation, University of Sussex].

Afanyi-Dadzie, E. (2019). Ban on caning will break down discipline in schools – methodist Bishop warns. *CITI Newsroom*. Retrieved February 8, 2020, from https://citinewsroom.com/2019/01/ban-on-caning-will-break-down-discipline-in-schools-methodist-bishop-warns/

Ajei, O. M. (2001). *Indigenous knowledge systems and good governance in Ghana: The traditional akan socio-political example* [Occasional dissertations No. 30, Institute of Economic Affairs].

Akyeampong, K. (2004).*Whole school development in Ghana* [Background dissertation, prepared for the Education for All Global Monitoring Report 2005 The Quality Imperative].

Akyeampong, K., & Stephens, D. (2002). Exploring the backgrounds and shaping of beginning student teachers in Ghana: Toward greater contextualisation of teacher education. *International Journal of Educational Development, 22,* 261–274.

Alhassan, A. B. (2013). School corporal punishment in Ghana and Nigeria as a method of discipline: A psychological examination of policy and practice. *Journal of Education and Practice, 4*(27), 137–147.

Ampadu, E., Butakor, P. K., & Cole, Y. (2017). Working together to improve the quality of mathematics education and students achievements: Exploring the views of Ghanaian parents. *African Research Review, 11*(1), 11–27.

Andrews, R. G. (2017). *A case study of parental involvement in basic education in rural Ghana* [Unpublished doctoral dissertation, University of Sussex].

Darvas, P., & Balwanz, D. (2014). *Basic education beyond the millennium development goals in Ghana: How equity in service delivery affects educational and learning outcomes.* World Bank Paper. World Bank. https://doi.org/10.1596/978-1-4648-0098-6

Donkor, A. (2010). Parental involvement in education in Ghana: The case of a private elementary school. *International Journal About Parents in Education, 4*(1), 23–28.

Essuman, A. (2013). *Decentralization of education management in Ghana: Key issues in school-community relations.* LAP LAMBERT Academic Publishing.

Essuman, A., & Akyeampong, K. (2011). Decentralisation policy and practice in Ghana: The promise and reality of community participation in education in rural community. *Journal of Education Policy, 26*(4), 513–527.

Foster, P. (1965). *Education and social change in Ghana.* University of Chicago Press.

Ghana Education Service. (2010). *Headteachers' handbook.* Ghana Education Service.

Ghana Education Service. (2012). *School management committee resource handbook.* Ghana Education Service.

Hedge, J. (2002). The importance of posting and interaction with the education bureaucracy in becoming a teacher in Ghana. *International Journal of Educational Development, 22,* 353–366.

Hirose, K. (2011). Chapter 25: Traditional chieftaincy. In T. Takane & S. Yamada (Eds.), *47 chapters to know Ghana.* Akashi Shoten.

Lartey, N. L. (2019). Ban on caning in order; it makes students timid' – GNECC. *CITI Newsroom.* Retrieved February 8, 2020, from https://citinewsroom.com/2019/01/ban-on-caning-in-order-it-makes-students-timid-gnecc/

McWilliam, H. O. A. (1957). *The development of education in Ghana.* Longmans.

Mfum-Mensah, O., & Friedson-Ridenour, S. (2014). Whose voices are being heard? Mechanism for community participation in education in Northern Ghana. *Prospects, 44,* 351–365.

Nishimura, M. (2017). Community participation in school management in developing countries. *Oxford Research Encyclopedia of Education.* https://doi.org/10.1093/acrefore/9780190264093.013.64

Nyanbor, J. (2019). GES reiterates ban on caning; directs new disciplinary methods. *CITI Newsroom.* Retrieved February 8, 2020, from https://citinewsroom.com/2019/01/ges-reiterates-ban-on-caning-directs-new-disciplinary-methods/

Pryor, J. (2005). Can community participation mobilize social capital for improvement of rural schooling? A case study from Ghana. *Compare, 35*(2), 193–203.

Sefa-Nyarko, C., Kyei, P., & Mwambari, D. (2018). *Background paper: Transitions from primary to lower secondary school: A focus on equity.* As Part of the Secondary Education in Africa: Preparing Youth for the Future of Work series (SEA) of MasterCard Foundation. Participatory Development Associate Ltd.

UNESCO Institute of Statistics. (n.d.). http://uis.unesco.org/en/country/gh

Volta Online. (2018). *Commercial use of motorbikes in Ghana; a convenient mode of transport or death trap?* Retrieved November 22, 2018, from https://voltaonlinegh.com/article-commercial-use-of-motorbikes-in-ghana-a-convenience-mode-of-transport-or-death-trap/

Yamada, S. (2011). History of Elite Education and Traditional Education. In Takane, T. & Yamada, S. (Eds.) *47 Chapters to Know Ghana.* Akashi Shoten.

4 Research method

Introduction

This chapter presents the conceptual framework of the study, which addresses the research gaps described in the literature review in relation to the research questions: (1) To what extent does community participation function in school management? (2) To what extent are community participation, SES, educational outcomes, and RT related? (3) How is RT realized between actors and in factors of school management to generate educational outcomes? This chapter deploys a mixed method to answer the research questions, and how data are collected and analyzed.

Conceptual framework

Based on the literature review, I developed a conceptual framework to consider the relationship among educational outcomes, actors, and factors in school management and RT.

First, in the quantitative analysis, I define educational outcomes as learning achievements measured by test scores for the sake of measuring its relationship with other variables. In the qualitative analysis, in addition to learning achievement, school enrollment and pupil discipline are also defined as educational outcomes. School enrollment appears as outcomes of school management because it is not the direct results of pedagogical efforts. However, as stated in Chapter 3 school enrollment can be a variable to signal guardian's good reputation of school quality. Pupil discipline appears as a key condition of education because the extent of pupils' discipline shows their readiness to learn and also guardians' support for pupils. However, as stated in Chapter 3, guardians and teachers expect pupils to be well disciplined as the outcomes of schooling. Thus, I include school enrollment and pupil discipline as educational outcomes in the qualitative analysis.

DOI: 10.4324/9781003320579-4

In the literature review, parents and community members have shifted from being supporters or inputs to decision-makers in school management. Under this context, I define school management to include school communities and parents, who were considered to be outside of school management. Subsequently, I decompose school management into managerial and pedagogical factors, as discussed in Byrk et al. (2010). Managerial factors include "Professional Capacity," "Parent, School, Community Ties," and "School Learning Climate." I did not include "Instructional Guidance" in the conceptual framework because it is difficult to determine how schools are aligned with curriculum within the limited time available through several field visits.

I define each factor as follows: "Professional Capacity" is defined as the extent to which schools have adequate quality and number of professional teachers, and whether teachers, including headteachers, have a common understanding as to how to achieve educational outcomes. "Parent, School, Community Ties" includes both collective participation as a member of school communities, and individual participation as individual parents. As collective participation appears to be an engine for school management in developing countries as described previously, it is worthwhile to examine to what extent school-level stakeholders participate in collective participation. "School Learning Climate" is regarded as the extent to which schools and classrooms in terms of school infrastructure are ready for teaching and learning. Then, "Pedagogical Factors" are considered as the extent of "Time for Learning," "Supplementary Resources," and "Dynamics of Student Learning" (composed of "Motivation" and "School Participation"). As teachers and pupils are part of this instructional triangle, I define motivation to include both "Teacher Motivation" and "Pupil Motivation."

Literature have argued that school-level stakeholders should work with children being at the centre of its relationship (Epstein et al., 2002; Sanders, 2002; Bryk & Schneider, 2002), so I assume that RT is realized with children being at the center of each relationship. RT operates in both managerial and pedagogical factors. As shown in the question items, "Teacher-parent RT" operates in managerial factors as information sharing, consultation with teachers, and through feeding breakfast. It operates in pedagogical factors by making sure that children attend school without delay or absence, providing needed items for schooling and looking after children's homework. "School communities-school RT" and "Headteacher-teacher RT" are also related to both managerial and pedagogical factors. For instance, mobilizing PTA funds is a managerial activity, whereas it also contributes to organizing extra classes for preparing students for the BECE. Headteachers and teachers discuss their relationship with school communities regarding how to improve pedagogical activities for children. In Figure 4.1, collective

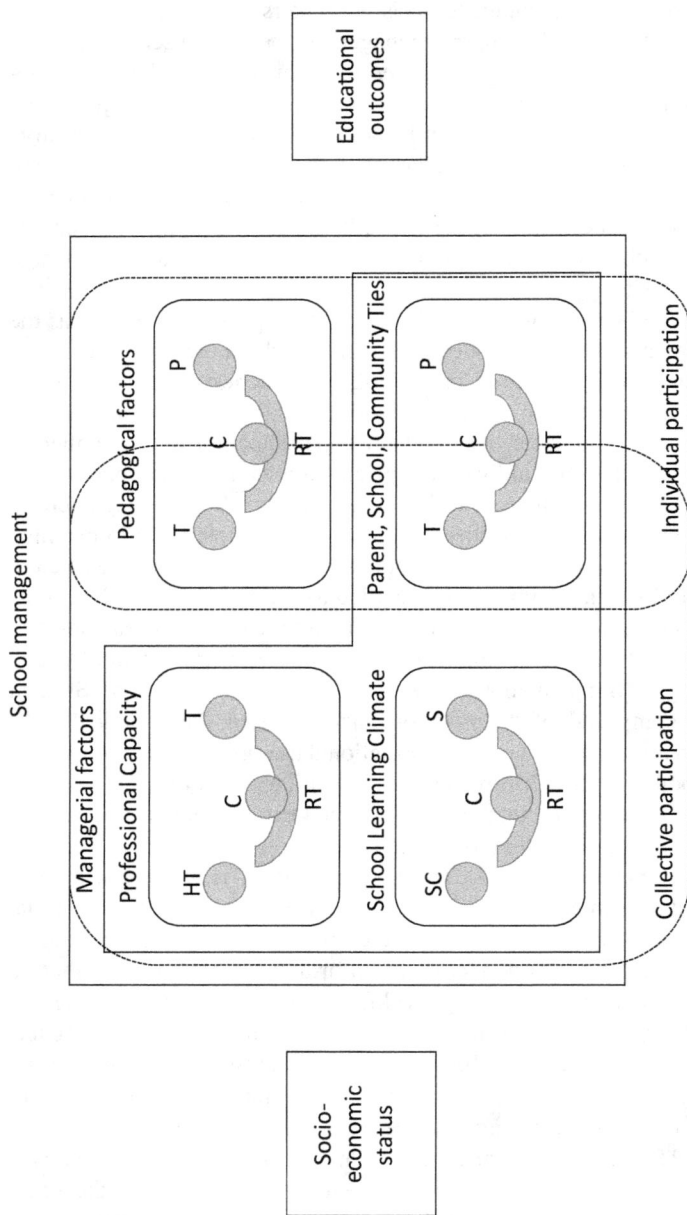

Figure 4.1 Conceptual framework

Note: In school management, circles and squares represent actors and factors respectively. RT denotes relational trust, which mediates between actors (SC: school communities, S: school, HT: headteacher, T: teacher, P: parent, C: children) and factors. Developed by the author.

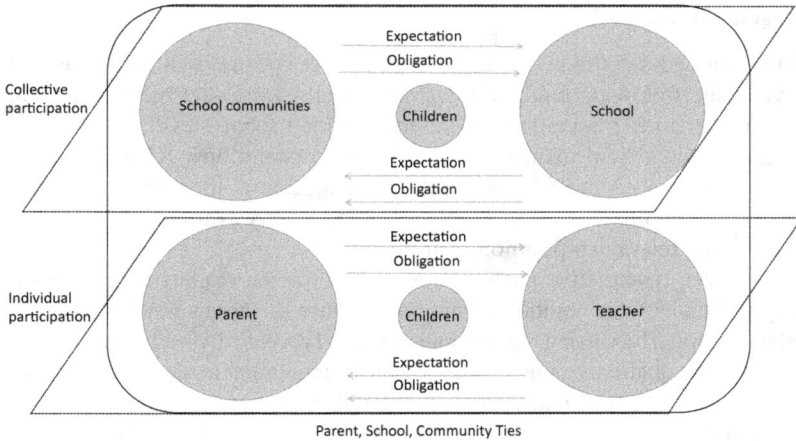

Figure 4.2 RT between school communities and school at collective participation and between parent and teacher at individual participation. Developed by the author.

and individual participation appears to overlap to some extent. As shown in Figure 4.2, they do not overlap horizontally, but rather vertically, because RT operates in a two-story arrangement of school management in collective and individual participation, respectively.

Figure 4.2 shows how RT between school communities and school, and teachers and parents, may or may not be realized in the "Parent, school, community ties" factor. Figure 4.2 also shows in detail how RT occurs as synchronies of mutual expectations and obligations. I pay special attention to RT between actors in each factor of school management and analyze how RT mediates managerial and pedagogical factors to produce educational outcomes.

Research questions

Based on the conceptual framework, I present the following research questions:

Research Question 1) To what extent does community participation function in school management?

Research Question 2) To what extent are community participation, SES, educational outcomes, and RT related?

Research Question 3) How is RT realized between actors and in factors of school management to generate educational outcomes?

Research method

This study adopts the mixed method to answer the research questions and reveals the following methodological research gaps in the literature. First, it is important to understand the extent to which school-level stakeholders participate in school management and to understand how RT affects educational outcomes and factors in school management, through quantitative analysis. With this, the readers can access objectively available data and can analyze the relationships among variables.

However, quantitative analysis does not allow the readers to understand why and under what realities RT has an influence on these variables and their relationships. Thus, using the qualitative study, I reveal why such relationships occur. In the qualitative study, I employ the triangulation method to determine the validity of the phenomenon using the following multiple sources of data: educational statistics, interview from different stakeholders, documentary data (SMC or PTA meeting minutes), and observations from the field visit.

Data collection

I present how the data collection instrument, data, and analytical method (Table 4.1) correspond to the research questions. First, to answer Research Question 1) To what extent do institutionalized school communities function? I collected data from the district education office and administered headteacher questionnaires. I conducted quantitative analysis (trend analysis and descriptive analysis).

Second, to answer Research Question 2) To what extent does RT affect educational outcomes and factors in school management? I collected data from the headteacher questionnaire and analyzed them using quantitative analysis (factor analysis, descriptive analysis, and correlational analysis).

Lastly, to answer Research Question 3) How does RT mediate managerial and pedagogical factors in school management to generate educational outcomes? I conducted qualitative analysis of how RT mediates managerial and pedagogical factors in school management, toward educational outcomes.

Data

In terms of educational outcomes, the BECE result is the most reliable and available source and it represents the only comparable data in terms of quality of education at the primary education level. School enrollment is affected by geographical location, (urban or rural), and SES (whether households are rich or poor). However, as discussed in the Chapter 3, school enrollment in rural areas is a measure of the reputation of schools owing to the activities in the schools. Thus, in this study, I consider school enrollment as one of the educational outcomes to be analyzed in the case study.

Table 4.1 Data source, data, and analytical method

Data source	Data				Analytical method
	SES	Community Participation	Relational trust	Educational outcomes	
District education office				✓	Trend analysis of the BECE ranking or mean aggregate and enrollment
Headteacher questionnaire (N = 85)	✓		✓		Factor analysis, descriptive analysis, correlational analysis
Brief headteachers' questionnaire (N = 50)					Descriptive analysis
Meeting minutes of SMC/PTA general/ executive meetings	✓		✓	✓	Qualitative analysis
Individual and focused-group interviews	✓		✓	✓	Qualitative analysis

Source: Author

It is common to use test scores or school enrollment as dependent vari-ables, as they are objectively available data, but it is difficult to investigate how children, as the subject of learning, are ready to learn. Pupil discipline reflects how children are motivated to learn, have self-esteem and respect for others. These are complex to be analyzed in quantitative study, thus I analyze pupil discipline as one of educational outcomes in the qualitative case study.

BECE

The results of the BECE can be described in the following ways. First, the pass rate shows how many pupils get below an aggregate of 30 in six sub-jects (aggregate five or below in each subject means a satisfactory level of attainment) among the applicants from each school. The pass rate does not mean the border line to determine their admission into SHSs. The pass rate fluctuates year by year because it is dependent on the number of applicants from each school. Even if the number of students obtaining an aggregate point below 30 is the same, when the number of applicants is smaller, the pass rate becomes higher. Thus, it does not necessarily mean that school performance is improving if the pass rate goes up. It requires cautions when comparing the pass rate over time.

Second, the BECE pass rate ranking is commonly used at the district level, when comparing the BECE results among schools. However, some schools can be the top at the same time because they achieved 100 percentage of pass rate. Despite such features, the BECE pass rate ranking shows the relative positions of schools in the district.

Lastly, the BECE results can be described as a mean aggregate. Although the pass rate is the same, it is possible to have different mean aggregates because of scores' distributions. Thus, it is relevant to use the mean aggregate to show accurately differences in the quality of education among schools and to analyze it quantitatively.

Enrollment

School enrollment data are normally collected every February and March through the Education Management Information System (EMIS) questionnaires. The district education office summarizes school enrollment by kindergarten, primary and JHS sections for all schools in a particular district. I collected school enrollment data from the summary table based on the EMIS questionnaires from the district education office.

Community participation

To assess the extent of community participation, I used the following data: frequency of PTA general meetings per year; average number of participants at PTA general meetings; PTA general meeting participation rate (the number of PTA general meeting participants compared to school enrollment); PTA funds collection rate (the number of those who paid against that of those who are supposed to pay); mobilized amount of PTA funds per year; mobilized amount of PTA funds per pupil; and number of mobilization channels. As the number of participants at PTA general meetings and mobilized amount of PTA funds depend on the number of school enrollment, it is necessary to avoid such bias.

Relational trust

I measure RT in both quantitative and qualitative ways. As discussed in the literature review, quantitative analysis of RT has the advantage of measuring the extent of RT and the relationships with educational outcomes and school management variables. Using the headteacher questionnaire, I collected data concerning the following role relationships: "School communities-school RT," "Headteacher-teacher RT" and "Teacher-teacher RT." I added "School communities-school RT," which is not available in the study of Byrk and Schneider (2002). I assume that school communities include SMC or PTA executive members, guardians and community members who attend SMC or PTA general meetings, whereas schools are represented by head-teachers and teachers.

When developing the question items for "Teacher-parent RT," I consider that parent participation may include both collective and individual participation, as mentioned in the Chapter 2. This is because parents partici-pate in collective spaces such as school meetings, but are also in charge of the day-to-day raising of their child/children at home. Thus, I realized that the collective aspect of parent participation could be captured in "School communities-school RT," whereas the individual aspect of parent participa-tion could appear as "Teacher-parent RT." I developed the question items of "Teacher-parent RT" accordingly.

Generally when developing the RT questionnaire, I referred to question items developed by Byrk and Schneider (2002) and Tsuyuguchi and Kura-moto (2014). The questions were classified into expectation and obligation items, except for "Teacher-teacher RT." The questionnaire uses a four-point Likert scale (4: strongly agree, 3: agree, 2: disagree, or 1: strongly disagree). I calculated the average score of the expectation and obligation items and multiplied both average scores to calculate the extent of RT, with reference to Tsuyuguchi and Kuramoto (2014).

Data collection instrument

Headteacher questionnaire

I developed a headteacher questionnaire to ask about 1) school and teacher profile, 2) the extent of community (collective) participation, and 3) the extent of RT between school communities and school, between teachers and parents, among teachers and between headteachers and teachers. The headteacher questionnaires were distributed to all 86 public basic schools in the Akatsi South District, through circuit supervisors at the district edu-cation office and 85 questionnaires were collected. See the details of the headteacher questionnaire in the Appendix 2.

Brief headteachers questionnaire

*I*n addition to the headteacher questionnaire, a brief headteacher question-naire was prepared and distributed to all the 86 public basic schools after the field survey in September 2017, in order to obtain socioeconomic data of schools. It contained a question regarding which geographical communities were feeding pupils into each school (at most five), based on the information from the 2010 Census. Out of the 86 questionnaire distributed, 50 were collected. See the questionnaire in the Appendix 3. To calculate SES for each school community, the 2010 Census data was used at the enumeration areas in the Akatsi South District. The enumeration areas were almost identical to the areas of geographical communities. To calculate SES, attention was given to the following data points: education level, economic activity, availability of drinking water and mobile phone ownership. More specifically, the followings data were employed: proportion of SHS graduates over community members who are over the age of 20; proportion of those who work in the agriculture sector; proportion of those who have access to sources of water that are not considered safe (unprotected well, river/stream, unprotected spring, dugout/pond/lake/dam/canal, or bore-hole/pump/tube well); and proportion of those who have mobile phones. The average of these feeding community' SES data were calculated and defined as school communities' SES.

Case study schools

During the field surveys, I visited seven public basic schools in the Akatsi South District. These seven schools were chosen as schools with high or low extent of community participation from the viewpoint of the district education officer who accompanied me during the field survey. I choose four schools as case study schools among these seven surveyed schools to answer Research Question 3.

Semi-structured, individual and focused group interview

Semi-structured and individual interviews were conducted for headteachers while semi-structured and focused group interviews were conducted for teachers, pupils and the SMC or PTA executive members. Details about the interviews and the interviewees are as shown in Tables 4.2, The headteachers were notified by the district education office of my visit and they arranged meetings with teachers, pupils and parents/guardians. During these interviews, the following questions were asked? How schools, school communities, and geographical communities worked in the past and at the present? What issues prevented or promoted educational outcomes for the school and relationships among pupils, parents, teachers, and headteachers? The interviews took place at the school compound and lasted from 30 minutes to one hour for each category of group. The interviews were conducted in English; a district education officer who accompanied me translated from Ewe, the local language, to English when the need arose.

Table 4.2 Interviews conducted during the field surveys (February and September 2017; September 2018)

No	School code in the text	Date	Interviewees
1	A20170925PU	Sep 25,2017	Primary grade six, 11 Pupils
2	A20170925PA	Sep 25,2017	12 adults (PTA chairman, SMC chief representative, head of town, PTA executive members (representative of mothers), parents), occupation: 10 out of 12 are farmer, sex (male (seven); female (five)), generation (30s (two), 40s (seven), 50s (two), 60s (one))
3	A20170925TC	25-Sep-17	Six teachers (male (three), female (three), qualification (government-hired (five), community-hired (one), educational background (Bachelor (two), Diploma (three), Senior High School (one), generation (20s (four), 30s (one), 40s (one))
4	A20170925HT	25-Sep-17	A male headteacher. Age (48), teaching experience 19 years, Deployed to this school in March 2017, the first schools as the headteacher, educational background (Bachelor)
5	A20180919PA	19-Sep-18	12 adults (PTA vice chairman, PTA treasure, SMC executive members. PTA executive members, parents), occupation: all except one trader are farmers, sex (male (seven); female (five))
6	A20180919TC	19-Sep-18	Six teachers (male (3) (note: one of them was a vice headteacher but he was promoted to headteacher in the new academic year and transferred to other school, but he was present at the time of interview), female (3) (two of them were not at this school last September)
7	A20180919HT	19-Sep-18	Same as in 2017
8	A20180924HT	24-Sep-18	Same as in 2017
9	A20180924PU	24-Sep-18	Primary grade six, four pupils (two male and two female)
10	B20170201	1-Feb-17	Three adults: Headmistress, SMC chair, SMC member (former headteacher) A female headteacher, Age: 40s, teaching experience: 19 years, deployed to this school as a headteacher in 2012, educational background: Bachelor

(*Continued*)

58   *Research method*

Table 4.2 (Continued)

No	School code in the text	Date	Interviewees
11	C20170922PA	22-Sep-17	Nine adults: Male (six), female (three); Age: 30s (one), 40s (four), 50s (two), 60s (one), 70s (one), Role description: Unit committee members (two), SMC chairman (one), SMC member (one), PTA chairman (one), town development committee chairman (one). parents (three); Occupation: farmer (seven), company employee (one)
12	C20170922TC	22-Sep-17	Nine teachers (JHS (three), primary (six); male (six), female (three); Age: 20s (three), 30s (four), 40s (one), 50s (one); educational background: Bachelor (one), Diploma (one), Teacher Training College (one)
13	C20170922HT	22-Sep-17	A male headteacher, Age: 53, teaching experience 21 years, serving as a headteacher of this school since 2013. Educational background: Teacher Training College
14	C20170922PU	22-Sep-17	JHS grade one, five pupils
15	D20170926PA	26-Sep-17	Three adults: Male (two), female (one); Age: 70s (one), 40s (one), 20s (one); Occupation: farmer (two); Educational background: Middle School Leaving Certificate (currently equivalent to Junior High School) (two) and Senior High School student (one).
16	D20170926TC	26-Sep-17	Two teachers. One male teacher (age 46, English language teacher at JHS, educational background: Certificate A post secondary); one female teacher (age 23, Primary grade five, educational background: Diploma in Basic education)
17	D20170926HT	26-Sep-17	A male headteacher, Age 43, teaching experience 18 years, serving as a headteacher of this school since 2014, Educational background: Bachelor.
18	D20180920PA	20-Sep-18	Six adults (Sex: male (four), female (two); Occupation: farmer (five), security (one); Role description: parent (one), PTA chairperson (one), SMC chairman (one), PTA executive member (one), SMC executive member (one), former PTA chairman (one).
19	D20180920TC	20-Sep-18	Same as in 2017
20	D20180920HT	20-Sep-18	Same as in 2017
21	D20180920PU	20-Sep-18	JHS grade three, three male and two female pupils

Source: Author

Review of documents/photos obtained through field study

Photographs of the available SMC or PTA general and executive meeting minutes were taken at the surveyed schools (Appendix 4). In case that these minutes were not available when I visited, I asked the district education officer to send me those minutes later as photo data via mobile phone application. All the meeting minutes were available in English, except for a few cases. The following photographs were also taken: the SRC, the SPIP, the EMIS school questionnaire, the Action plans for the term (which specified school activities held in the term), the school time table, the teacher attendance check list, the submission list of scheme of work, the lesson notes which had been vetted by a headteacher and other materials such as coaching observation tools. I also took photos that showed the school atmosphere including school infrastructure and equipment.

To avoid the possibility of respondent bias, the triangulation methodology was adopted. When analyzing data, without referring to a single source of information, several sources were used to avoid subjective impressions from the interviewees. For instance, if quotes made by parents were referred, quotes from headteachers, teachers and pupils were obtained on the same matter, to validate the response from parents.

When conducting interviews, I referred to the SMC or PTA meeting minutes or observation (photo records) during the field visit. This enabled me to trace back the past discussion at school communities, to know how issues have been discussed in a chronological manner, and to validate the statement with the documents or physical evidence.

Negotiating access

I have worked for the Japan International Cooperation Agency (JICA) and had stayed in Ghana from 2002 to 2005, engaging with a joint project implemented by JICA and GES. With such background, I have contacts with JICA as well as the GES headquarters. First, a JICA expert, whom I have known beforehand, was contacted because she worked for the GES headquarter as an adviser on education decentralization. Through the consultation, the Akatsi South District in the Volta region, one of two pilot districts of JICA-supported community participation interventions, was selected as the field cite. This was because the District Director of Education showed commitment to accepting my research in this field, thus I could expect cooperation from the district education office to the extent that was possible.

Prior to each field survey, research permissions were given to enable me to conduct field studies in the Akatsi South district. When starting the field survey, I explained the objectives of the field study to the District Director of Education in the Akatsi South District. Through the consultation, surveyed schools were selected and the school visit was scheduled by the district education office. Circuit supervisors supported me with the collection of the headteacher questionnaire. The results of the field survey were reported to the Director of Education (Akatsi South District), the Regional Director of Education (Volta region), and officers at the Basic Education Division at the GES headquarters.

In terms of statistical data, I contacted the Ghana Statistical Service Headquarters and got permission to use the Population and Housing Census 2010 data of the Akatsi South District. In terms of budget and school construction data, I contacted the DA at the Akatsi South District and collected the necessary information.

Researcher identification

I was introduced to stakeholders of the visited schools as a researcher from Hiroshima University, Japan. No reference was made to the fact that I had worked for JICA, and it was unlikely that headteachers who answered the questionnaire and the interviewees would have perceived me as somebody from JICA, one of the development partners in Ghana. As I am a foreigner, it is difficult to avoid bias whereby respondents may overemphasize the necessity of external support, considering the affirmative nature of Ghanaians.

Ethical consideration

In terms of ethical consideration, the headteacher questionnaire stipulated that the information gathered through the questionnaire will be strictly used for this research only, and that individual information would not be revealed to the public. In addition, pseudonyms were used for the targeted schools, and the interviewed participants were kept anonymous. When interviewees mentioned somebody else's names in an interview, these names were made pseudonyms for privacy purpose. Schools' names and stakeholders' names in the photos were also made pseudonyms.

Data analysis

Quantitative analysis

Descriptive analysis of community participation was conducted based on the headteacher's questionnaire. To identify whether the indicators in each RT could be classified as expected, factor analysis was employed for each RT. Then, correlation analysis was made among educational outcomes, SES, community participation and RT. To avoid correlations among these variables, principal component analysis was conducted to simplify key variables such as SES, community participation and RT, and calculated their composite indicators. Educational outcomes here are defined as the BECE mean aggregate, because this is comparable among schools in terms of the quality of education.

Qualitative analysis

To analyze the qualitative data such as interviews and documents, the MAXQDA18, a software program was utilized. This software provides the following four displays: "document system," where all the inputted meeting minutes and interview transcripts were listed; "code system" to describe the codes that I adopted following the conceptual framework; "document browser," which shows the details of the documents activated in document system, and finally, "retrieved segments," which shows all of the segments in the activated documents that can be classified by activated codes.

Deductive coding was adopted based on the conceptual framework and the codes were placed in the "code system." These codes include one corresponding to pedagogical factors in school management: "Pupils' motivation (pupils' discipline)" and "Teachers' motivation"; managerial factors in school management: "Parent, School, Community Ties" (school finance, parents' support, and collective participation) and "School learning climate" (learning environment and school infrastructure).

Finally, the above-mentioned codes were examined to analyze whether each of "School communities-school RT," "Headteacher-teacher RT," "Teacher-parent RT," and "Teacher-teacher RT" were realized as synchronies in mutual expectations and obligations. To show whether RT is realized, the following definition was utilized: when communications, consultations and decision-making are made regarding actions to solve issues, this is regarded as the expansion of "expectations." If resources are mobilized to respond to such expectations, it suggests that "obligations" are being made. Synchronies in expectations and obligations are not necessarily observed as instant phenomena. This requires time-series analysis to determine whether decisions made at the previous general meeting have been put into practice at the following general meeting.

References

Bryk, A. S., & Schneider, B. (2002). *Trust in schools: A core resource for improvement*. Russell Sage Foundation.

Bryk, A. S., Sebring, P. B., Allensworth, E., Luppescu, S., & Easton, J. Q. (2010). *Organizing schools for improvement: Lessons from Chicago*. University of Chicago Press.

Epstein, J. L., Sanders, M. G., Simon, B. S., Salinas, K. C., Jansorn, N. R., & Van Voorhis, F. L. (2002). *School, family, and community partnerships: Your handbook for action* (2nd ed.). Corwin Press Inc., A Sage Publications Company.

Sanders, M. G. (2002). Community involvement in school improvement: The little extra that makes a big difference. In J. L. Epstein, M. G. Sanders, B. S. Simon, K. C. Salinas, N. R. Jansorn, & F. L. Van Voorhis (Eds.), *School, family, and community partnerships: Your handbook for action* (2nd ed.). Corwin Press Inc., A Sage Publications Company.

Tsuyuguchi, K., & Kuramoto, T. (2014). Parent networks as determinants of relational trust. *Bulletin of the Faculty of Education, Ehime University, 61,* 57–69.

5 Findings about how relational trust works

Introduction

This chapter reveals the findings that answer the research questions through both quantitative and qualitative research methods. First, this chapter analyzes the trends of educational outcomes in the Akatsi South District to understand an overall picture of the district. Second, the chapter presents findings from the quantitative research and discusses its implications. Finally, the chapter explains the results of the qualitative analysis of three case studies, which compare two schools with similar backgrounds but different levels in the following educational outcomes: BECE, school enrollment, and pupils' discipline.

Status quo of educational outcomes in the Akatsi South District

BECE

The BECE mean aggregate data for each school were only available from 2016 to 2017. As mentioned in the previous section of the book, the BECE pass rate fluctuates over time. Thus, the BECE district ranking was useful for understanding the relative positions and the trends over years in the district. Generally, newly established private schools and public schools in urban areas tend to achieve higher levels in the BECE rankings, whereas public basic schools in rural areas have shown declining rankings over time.

Enrollment

The Akatsi South District has the following school enrollment in 2017/2018; KG: 4,612, primary: 11,915; and JHS: 416, while in 2015, there were 4,442

DOI: 10.4324/9781003320579-5

for KG, 11,917 for primary, and 3,990 for JHS. This means that there were some increases in enrollment in KG (170), primary (2) though insignificant, and JHS (177). Except for schools with only KG or JHS sections, public schools can be categorized by their size as follows: below 100 (15.19%), above 100 and below 250 (45.57%), and above 250 (39.24%). As shown in Chapter 3, primary education in Ghana is largely delivered by small- and medium-sized schools. The case of the Akatsi South District shows that their school enrollment is far lower than the national average. There tends to be higher enrollment in KG than in the primary section. If basic schools have only 100 students enrolled, with two KG and six primary classes (one class for one grade) and one teacher is assigned to each class, the teacher-to-pupil ratio would be approximately 1 to about 12, which is far less than the district average of 27 in 2017/2018 (stipulated in the district profile of the Annual School Census). Among the 31 schools with enrollment above 250, 12 were located in urban areas, representing the majority of 18 urban public schools in the district. In summary, schools with larger enrollment tend to be located in urban areas, whereas those with smaller enrollment are more common in rural areas.

School enrollment is a critical indicator for school management. It is possible that schools with lower enrollment may face challenges of inactive lessons owing to lower enrollment and have limited resources for school management. For example, because the government CG is distributed per capita according to school enrollment, those with higher enrollment will get more funds from the CG. In case of basic schools without JHS sections, pupils have to go and attend JHS in nearby communities.

Findings from community participation in school management

Institutionalized school communities' participation

Based on the headteacher questionnaire, the status quo of institutionalized community participation (SMC meetings, development of SPIP, disbursement of CG, and organization of SPAM) was revealed as follows (Tables 5.1 and 5.2).

First, the headteacher questionnaire showed that SMCs and PTAs organized their general and executive meetings jointly: SMC and PTA executive meetings (86.2%) and SMC and PTA general meetings (90.6%). This shows that although SMC and PTA are different organizations, most of the members representing the various stakeholders overlap and these two bodies operate in tandem. Therefore, this study refers them as SMC/PTA. While executive meetings are for institutionalized participation by SMC/PTA executive

Table 5.1 Descriptive statistics of educational outcomes, socioeconomic status, collective participation, and RT

		District average	SD
Educational outcomes	BECE mean aggregate (2017)	33.12	6.47
	Number of pupils (2016)	232.61	154.95
Relational trust	School community–school RT	10.8	2.25
	Teacher–parent RT	9.62	2.53
	Headteacher–teacher RT	12.36	2.4
	Teacher-teacher RT	3.41	0.38
Collective participation	Average participant number	65.23	37.91
	PTA general meeting participation rate (%) (2016)	35	19
	Amount of mobilized PTA levy (GHC) (2016)	543.84	671.9
	Average amount of PTA levy per enrollment (GHC) (2016)	1.91	1.56
	Number of resource mobilization channels (2016)	5.52	2
Socioeconomic status	Proportion of those graduated from Senior High School and above (%)	11.85	4.96
	Proportion of agriculture industry (%)	68.76	18.27
	Proportion of those who have access to water sources that are not considered safe	68.82	26.47
	Proportion of those who have mobile phone (%)	28.15	8.82

Source: Author based on the 2010 Housing and Population Census (SES) and the headteacher questionnaire (85 samples, SES, collective participation, RT), and the Akatsi South District education office (educational outcomes)

Note: District average and SD (standard deviation) are for 85 public basic schools in the Akatsi South District

Table 5.2 Descriptive statistics of institutionalized participation in school management

Development of SPIP	Every year without delay	Every year but with delay	Not every year	Not at all
	49.4%	33.73%	14.46%	2.41%
Scope of stakeholders to discuss SPIP (multiple answers)	Discuss with school staff	Discuss with SMC chairperson	Discuss with SMC or PTA executive members	Discuss with parents and community members at SMC or PTA general meetings
	81.2%	74.1%	52.9%	18.8%
Timing of disbursement of CG	Just when SPIP activities start	Nearly half of way in the implementation of SPIP activities	When SPIP activities are going to end	After SPIP activities end or later
	17.7%	16.5%	11.4%	54.4%

Source: Headteacher questionnaire

members who discuss and endorse the SPIP, general meetings were spaces for consensual democracy, which parents and community members have adapted from the traditional chieftaincy practices. Thus, school communities in Ghana exist as hybrids between institutionalized executive members and parents/indigenous geographical communities members.

The average number of participants for SMC/PTA general meetings was 65.23, and the average amount of PTA funds mobilized at meetings was GHC543.84 in 2016. Whereas the institutionalized school communities' participation emphasizes representative democracy, participation in general meetings, and the collection of PTA funds as voluntary contributions are still functioning. The SMC/PTA general meeting participation rate in 2016 was 35% (the average number of participants in PTA general meetings against the number of children enrolled in school). Parents or guardians may have more than one child in the school; however, it was difficult to calculate the number of households accurately; thus, this is a rough estimation of meeting participation rate. The PTA funds collection rate in 2016 was 63% (those who paid PTA funds against those who are supposed to pay). This shows that, except for the CG, there exists a certain level of collective participation in the communities toward schools' development. It is however important to note that not all guardians and community members participate in meetings or pay PTA funds.

The extent of institutionalized participation in school management in the Akatsi South District is shown in Table 5.2. In terms of the development of the SPIP, those who answered had the following responses: "every year without delay" (49.4%), "every year but with delay" (33.73%), "not every year" (14.46 percentage), and "not at all" (2.41%). This means that the majority of schools (83.13%) developed the SPIP every year. In addition, in terms of the question (multiple answers) about the scope of discussions before submission of the SPIP to the district education office, responses were as follows: "discuss with school staff" (81.2%), "discuss with SMC chairperson" (74.1%), "discuss with SMC or PTA executive members" (52.9%), and "discuss with parents and community members at SMC or PTA general meetings" (18.8%). This shows that most schools discuss SPIP with teachers, the SMC chairperson, and SMC or PTA executive members. However, they do not discuss with parents and community members at PTA or SMC general meetings.

Regarding the disbursement timing of the CG, the results were as follows: "just when SPIP activities start" (17.7%), "nearly half of way into the implementation of SPIP activities" (16.5%), "when SPIP activities are going to end" (11.4%), and "after SPIP activities end or later" (54.4%). Moreover, the district average of SPAM was 1.35 meeting per year. In summary, most schools developed a SPIP; however, its scope of discussion was limited to SMC or PTA executive members, and the disbursement of CG was seriously delayed. The notice from the district education office dated September 17, 2017 indicated that the first and second batch of the disbursement of the CG into the school account in 2016/2017 academic year, starting September 2016, were delayed for almost 1 year (Figure 5.1).

The disbursement of the CG is intended to trigger activities planned in the SPIP, and the results of activities are reviewed in the SPAMs or SMC/PTA general meetings. However, institutionalized community participation has flaws because its intended process does not work as data indicate. SMC resource handbook (Ghana Education Service, 2012) recommends that schools need to encourage all stakeholders to show interest and participate in the planning of the SPIP (p61). However, the results showed that the involvement of stakeholders in the SPIP development was limited to mainly headteachers, school staff, SMC chairpersons, or executive members (Figure 5.2). The disbursement of the CG, which is an engine to move the planned SPIP activities forward, was often delayed. This made it difficult for school communities to hold schools accountable, because the necessary support or resources were not available for schools to make activities/actions happen.

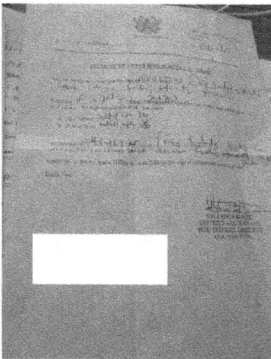

Figure 5.1 Notification letter from the district education office in terms of the capitation grant disbursement to school account. Photograph by the author.

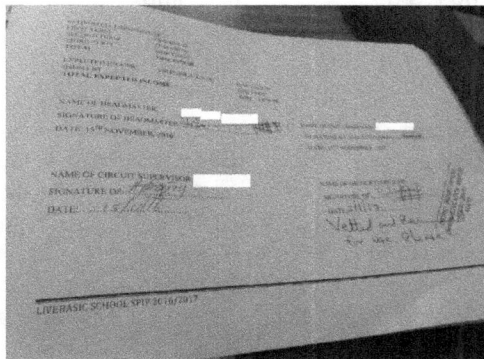

Figure 5.2 School Performance Improvement Plan signed by headteacher, SMC chairperson, and circuit supervisor in charge. Photograph by the author.

Findings of the extent to which RT affects educational outcomes and factors in school management

Factor analysis and reliability test of RT

I conducted factor analysis for each RT to identify which factors determined each question item (see Appendix 5). First, in terms of "School communities-school RT," I conducted factor analysis (principal axis factoring method, Promax rotation). I hypothesized that two factors, namely, expectations and obligations, would be present in "School communities-school RT." The scree plot showed the possibility of two factors. As a result of factor analysis, I found two factors and named them "expectation" factor (SC12, SC10, SC11, SC9, SC14, SC5, SC7, and SC13) and "obligation' factor" (SC18, SC15, SC17, SC20, and SC19). SC16 was excluded from the expectation factor because its factor loading was .376 and because the question item did not fit the expectation factor. I also conducted a reliability test and calculated the Cronbach's alpha for the expectation factor (.786) and the obligation factor (.812).

Likewise, I conducted factor analysis (principal axis factoring method, Promax rotation) for "Teacher-parent RT." Based on a scree plot, two factors were identified. I named one factor the "expectation" factor (TPR4, TPR1, TPR3, TPR2, TPR6, TPR5, and TPR7) and the other factor as the "obligation" factor (TPR9, TPR11, TPR13, TPR10, TPR12, TPR14, and TPR8). I also conducted the reliability test and the Cronbach's alpha for the expectation factor (.882) and the obligation factor (.729).

In terms of "Headteacher-teacher RT," I conducted factor analysis (principal axis factoring method, promax rotation), and based on the scree plot, the two factors were identified. I named one factor as the "expectation" factor (HTR3, HTR4, HTR1, HTR2, and HTR5) and the other factor as the "obligation" factor (HTR10, HTR6, HTR11, and HTR9). I also conducted the reliability test and the Cronbach's alpha for the expectation factor (.802) and the obligation factor (.626). See Appendix 5 for the results of the factor analysis.

Descriptive analysis

Relational trust

After factor analysis, the score of the "School communities-school RT," "Teacher-parent RT," and "Headteacher-teacher RT" was calculated by multiplying the average of the expectation factor and the obligation factor. In the case of the "Teacher-teacher RT," the score was calculated by averaging all the question items. The descriptive statistics of RT is shown in Appendix 6. Several question items showed the ceiling effects, meaning that the answers were skewed to the right (4: strongly agree). This is because this study adopted measuring RT from the perspective of headteachers. Head-teachers' responses, represented by each school, had little variance, and this might have caused a ceiling effect.

Generally, the average "Teacher-parent RT" was relatively low, com-pared to the other RTs. This is because the expectation factor had a lower score than the others. For instance, the following questions had low scores: "Parents look after children's homework at home or secure their learning time at home" (2.4), "Parents make sure that children come to school with-out any delay or absence" (2.61), and "Parents provide breakfast for chil-dren to let them be active for school activities" (2.73). This implied that teachers had lower expectations for parents in terms of learning at home, enrolling in schools, and basic child raising at home.

The obligation factors scored higher than expectation factors in both "School communities-school RT" and "Teacher-parent RT." This might have been because headteachers tended to defend the idea that schools and teachers were performing their expected duties. In terms of "School communities-school RT," the following question had the lowest score among all items: "School communities provide necessary support for teachers" (2.54). This implies that, from the viewpoint of headteachers, school communities are not likely to provide support for teachers.

Socioeconomic status

The district average of the proportion of SHS graduates over community mem-bers who were over the age 20 was 11.86%, for those who worked for agri-culture was 68.76%, those who had access to sources of water that were not considered safe was 68.82%, and those who had mobile phone was 28.15%.

Correlation among educational outcomes, SES, collective participation, and RT

The results of correlational analysis are shown in Appendix 7. Variables in SES, collective participation, and RT were likely to be correlated to each other. Therefore, to avoid such correlations among the same variable cate-gories, the analytical model was made simple. For the sake of that, the prin-cipal component analysis was conducted and the composite variables were created for community participation (collective participation), SES, and RT.

In the correlation analysis, the following was found. First, the SES composite variable was correlated with the BECE mean aggregate (2017) (coefficient = −.413, p < .05) (Figure 5.3). This means that pupils at well-endowed school communities tended to have higher learning outcomes, as suggested in the literature.

In my hypothesis, the larger the extent of RT, the lower the BECE mean aggregate (the higher the learning outcomes). Contrary to this hypothesis, it is only "Teacher-parent RT" that was correlated with the BECE mean aggregate (coefficient is −.471, p < .01) (Figure 5.4). Considering the results of the correlation analysis, the following question emerged: why do schools with similar SES have different levels of attainment in terms of the BECE and how will "Teacher-parent RT" will affect BECE in the process?

Second, the SES composite variable was correlated with school enrollment (primary school section, in 2017) (coefficient = .525, p < .01) (Figure 5.5). This implied that when household's SES tended to be higher, school enrollment also increases. This might be because larger-sized schools are often located in urban areas, where SES is generally higher.

In addition, the collective participation composite variable was correlated with school enrollment (primary school section) (coefficient = .503, p < .05) (Figure 5.6). This means that school enrollment formed the basis of collective participation. If school enrollment would be larger, the number of participants in the meetings and the amount of mobilized PTA funds would also be larger.

It was found that "School communities-school RT" was correlated with the collective participation composite variable (coefficient = .372, p < .05) (Figure 5.7). Among the "School communities-school RT," the expectation factor was correlated with the collective participation composite variable (coefficient = .490, p < .01). This means that the higher expectations schools have for

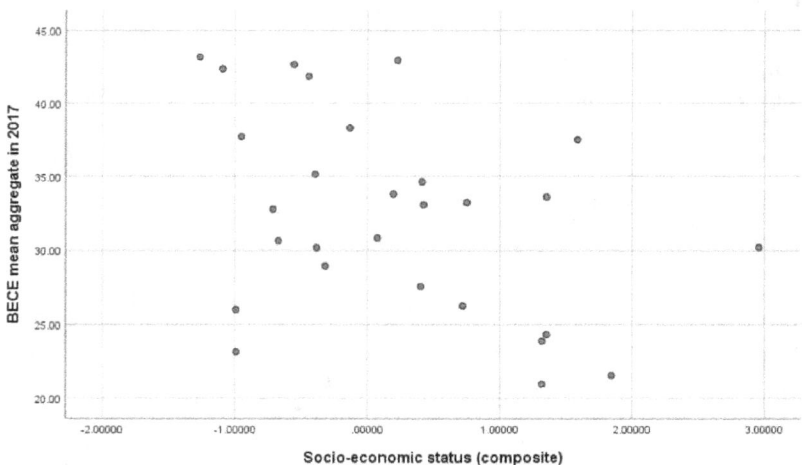

Figure 5.3 Scatter plot between socioeconomic status (composite) and BECE mean aggregate in 2017. Developed by the author.

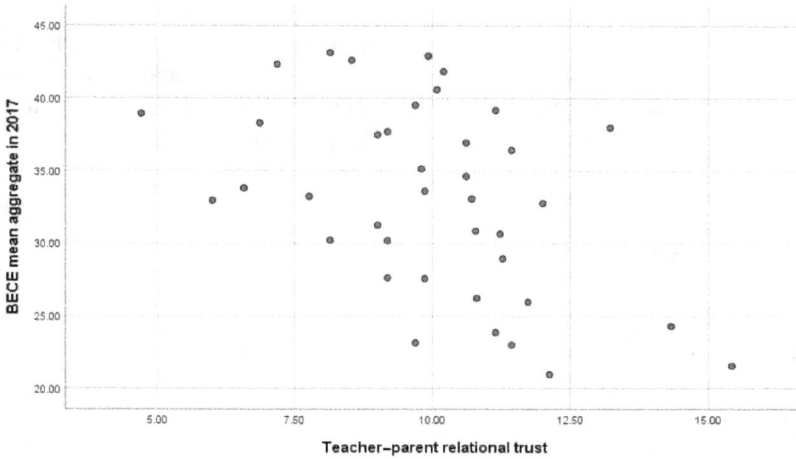

Figure 5.4 Scatter plot between teacher–parent RT and BECE mean aggregate in 2017. Developed by the author.

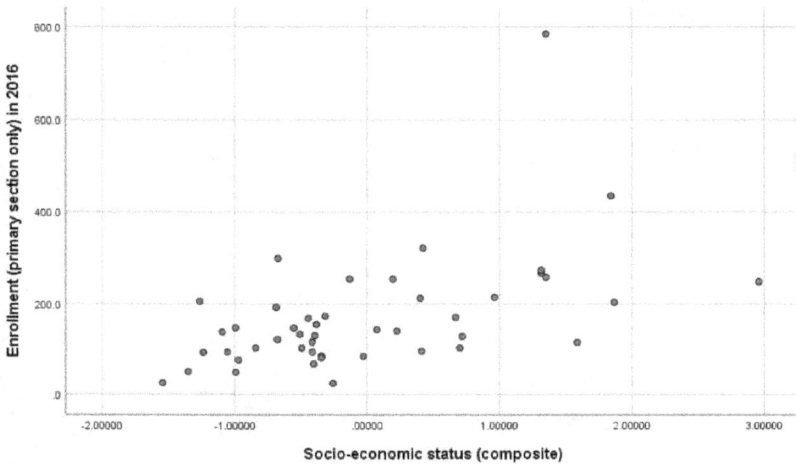

Figure 5.5 Scatter plot between socioeconomic status (composite) and enrollment (primary school section) in 2016. Developed by the author.

their school communities, the larger the extent of collective participation that would be available.

The results of correlation analysis can be interpreted as follows. First, a certain level of school enrollment is vital for sustaining community participation and vice-versa. Without a number of school enrollment, the population that can engage in community /parent participation is limited.

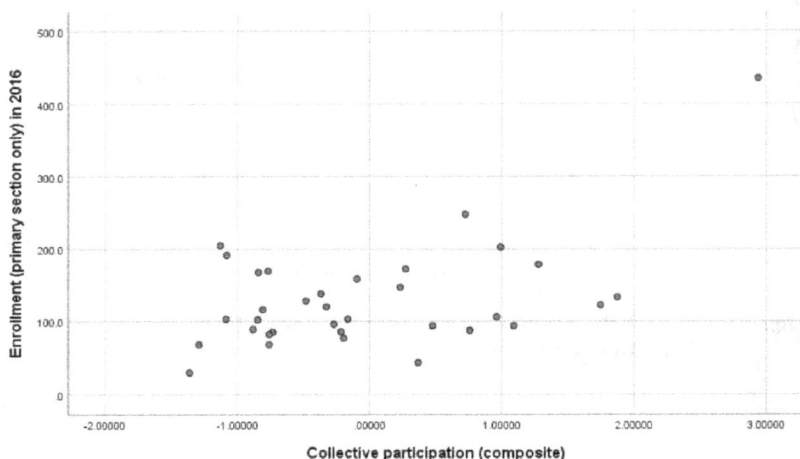

Figure 5.6 Scatter plot between collective participation (composite) and enrollment (primary school section) in 2016. Developed by the author.

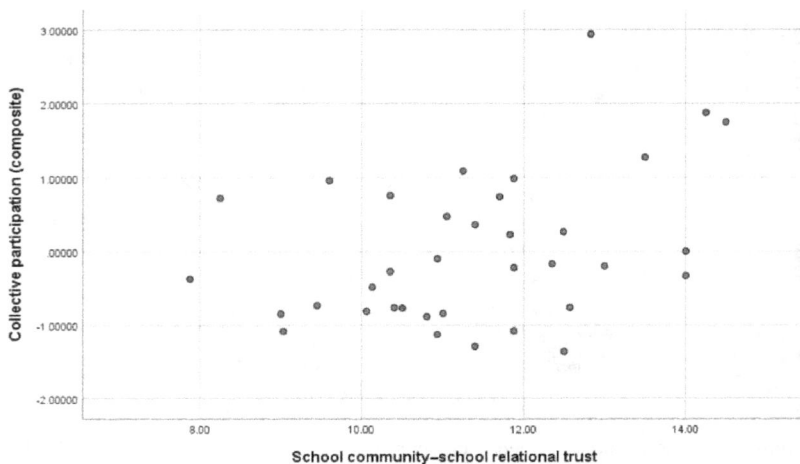

Figure 5.7 Scatter plot between school communities–school RT and collective participation (composite). Developed by the author.

Also, without some extent of collective participation, it is difficult to attract other parents/pupils to join the school. Second, I hypothesized that "School communities-school RT" would be correlated with learning outcomes and collective participation, because their collective support for school development is vital to improving pupils' learning environment. The results showed that "School communities-school RT" was correlated with the collective participation composite variable but not with learning outcomes. This may suggest that "School communities-school RT" or collective participation alone do not necessarily lead to improved learning outcomes but rather the connection between the managerial factor (collective participation) and the pedagogical factor is necessary. Third, it was a new finding that "Teacher-parent RT," which I assumed to deal with individual participation by parents/guardians at home, was correlated with learning outcomes. Thus, further in-depth studies are needed to determine the other factors affecting their relationship through the regression analysis, and to determine why and under what realities they are correlated, through the qualitative analysis.

Considering that SES was correlated with school enrollment, the following question emerged: Why was it that the higher the collective participation, the higher the school enrollment? Furthermore, why was it that the higher the "School communities-school RT," the higher the collective participation? This is particularly significant in rural areas, where SES is low and school enrollment is limited, compared to urban schools.

Summary and position of case study schools in the Akatsi South District

The following question emerged as the result of the quantitative study: Why do some schools have better educational outcomes than others with the same background? Thus, three case studies were conducted to answer why such situations occur, by presenting case studies that compared two schools with similar backgrounds but different educational outcomes.

(BACKGROUND)

School A   School A was established in 1946. It is located 30 minutes by car from the town center of Akatsi. To reach this school, it is necessary to go along an unpaved road from the main road for 25 minutes and only local residents would use such narrow roads for daily transportation. There was a school welcome signboard with a pupils' picture at the junction near the school. Farming is the main source of work in this area. The geographical communities established the school's basic structure with clay walls and provided labor and levied money from community members/parents for the

Table 5.3 Descriptive statistics of case study schools

		District average	SD	School A	School B	School C	School D
Educational outcomes	BECE mean aggregate (2017)	33.12	6.47	–	–	28.96	42.61
	School enrollment (2016)	232.61	154.95	220	89	303	365
Relational trust	School community–school relational trust	10.8	2.25	11.88	12	12.49	10.93
	Teacher–parent relational trust	9.62	2.53	10.71	9.23	10.95	8.53
	Headteacher–teacher RT	12.36	2.4	13.5	16	9	12.8
	Teacher–teacher relational trust	3.41	0.38	3.38	3.88	3.13	3.13
Collective participation	Average participant number at PTA general meetings (2016)	65.23	37.91	53.33	28	68	35
	PTA general meeting participation rate (2016) (%)	35	19	24	31	22	10
	Amount of mobilized PTA levy (2016) (GHC)	543.84	671.9	160	–	1,135	130
	Average amount of PTA levy per enrollment (2016) (GHC)	1.91	1.56	0.73	–	3.75	0.36
	Number of resource mobilization channels (2016)	5.52	2	6	2	3	5
Socioeconomic status	Proportion of those who graduated from Senior High School and above (%)	11.85	4.96	8.93	–	12.47	11.59
	Proportion of agriculture industry (%)	68.76	18.27	69.63	–	82.28	80.49
	Proportion of those who have access to water sources that are not considered safe (5) (%)	68.82	26.47	88.98	–	91.35	84.8
	Proportion of those who have mobile phone (%)	28.15	8.82	29.06	–	30.76	22.14

Source: Author based on the 2010 Housing and Population Census (SES) and the headteacher questionnaire (SES, collective participation, RT), and the Akatsi South District education office (educational outcomes)

Note: District average and SD (standard deviation) are for 85 public basic schools in the Akatsi South District.

school's construction. It has KG and primary sections with a total enroll-ment of 220 in 2016. The low level of school enrollment has been a major concern for school communities because it is a bottleneck for requesting the district education office to have a junior high school at the school compound.

School B   School B was established in 1989. It is located 30 minutes by car from the town center and along the main road. There were only three classrooms, in addition to the headteacher's office. Multigrade teaching is conducted at this school, owing to the limited number of pupils. There was a dispute among the village concerning the school's location. A group sug-gested that the school should be built in the middle of the village, but due to this being an area at risk of flooding, it was agreed to be located at its current place. This caused a long-lasting dispute, however, and 10 years ago, the village festival (durbar) stopped. It has KG and primary sections with the total enrollment of 89 in 2016.

School C   School C was established in 1952. It is located 4.5 km away from the main/paved road. Electricity is available at this school. The main ethnic group in these schools' geographical communities is the Ewe. Most of the community members are farmers. Five to six geographical communi-ties feed pupils to School C. These geographical communities discussed the needs of establishing the school and built the foundation structure before the government came in. The Member of Parliament of the Akatsi South District is from this community. They lobbied and established a three-unit classroom block using the DA Common Funds. It has KG, primary, and JHS sections with a total enrollment of 303 in 2016.

School D   School D was established in 1935; it is one of the oldest schools in the district. The first District Commissioner (currently the District Chief Exec-utive) of the District was from this community. It is located in a rural area, and it takes 20 minutes by car to reach it from the town center. According to the headteacher, its community members are mostly indigenous people, unlike in Akatsi town, where the people comprise a mix of different origins. This school serves 14–20 geographical communities, which have several chiefs. Dispute over the chieftaincy occurred in 2013 because two chiefs quarreled over the position of the paramount chief, which divided all the communities. Owing to the dispute, their traditional festival has attracted only a handful of people. It has KG, primary, and JHS sections with the total enrollment of 365.

BECE   Regarding the BECE pass rate ranking, the performances of Schools C and D were relatively good compared to other schools in rural areas in 2013 (13th for School C and 19th for School D). However, they showed different trends after 2013. School D was ranked sixth among public basic schools in rural areas, showing that School D was relatively better off in terms of the BECE pass rate ranking. However, private schools have emerged and have recently occupied the upper ranking; thus, the ranking of public schools has declined as a whole after 2017. In addition, while School D was ranked 50th, School C still held a better ranking than others in rural areas. This showed that these two schools developed a sharp contrast in terms of the differences in their BECE pass rare ranking.

The far-right column of Table 5.4 shows the extent to which the BECE ranking has declined over time in comparison between 2013 and the average

Table 5.4 BECE pass rate rank league table in the Akatsi South District (2013–2017) and the rank of School C and School D

School/Year	2013(A)	2014	2015	2016	2017	Average (2014–2017) (B)	(A)-(B)
School 1	31	37	39	39	46	40.3	-9.3
School 2	10	24	22	29	23	24.5	-14.5
School 3	23	31	40	28	26	31.3	-8.3
School 4	26	29	35	34	42	35.0	-9.0
School 5	36	40	27	44	13	31.0	5.0
School C	13	8	23	26	34	22.8	-9.8
School 7	29	36	28	32	41	34.3	-5.3
School 8	20	11	26	24	22	20.8	-0.8
School 9	32	25	15	46	44	32.5	-0.5
School 10	34	22	37	25	37	30.3	3.8
School 11	-	27	38	20	21	26.5	0.5
School 12	18	28	8	27	43	26.5	-8.5
School 13	25	34	36	41	14	31.3	-6.3
School 14	24	39	17	36	40	33.0	-9.0
School 15	22	26	33	42	36	34.3	-12.3
School D	19	17	29	40	50	34.0	-15.0
School 17	37	32	41	45	51	42.3	-5.3
School 18	33	35	34	30	49	37.0	-4.0
School 19	30	18	25	19	31	23.3	6.8
School 20	38	30	30	31	52	35.8	2.3
School 21	12	14	24	38	19	23.8	-11.8
School 22	16	21	12	21	27	20.3	-4.3
School 23	-	-	5	4	17	8.7	-3.7

Source: Author based on data from the Akatsi South District Education office

Note 1: Figures show the rank of each school in terms of the BECE pass rate. The higher the pass rate is, the smaller the number of rank is.

Note 2: Negative figures on the far right column mean that the position has declined in comparison between the 2013 and the average of 2014–2017, whereas positive figures mean the opposite.

Note 3: Columns with NA mean that no data was available.

between 2014 and 2017. The negative figures in this column show that the ranking declines from 2013 in the view of the average of 2014–2017. As shown in Table 5.4, ranking goes up and down every year and it is not feasible to compare the ranking in two points, for instance, 2013 and 2017. Therefore, I calculated the average of ranking between 2013 and 2016 and compared it with that in 2017 when I conducted the field survey. This is to show the general trend between 2013 and 2017 in the BECE pass rate ranking though ranking fluctuates every year.

School enrollment   School enrollment depends on the number of children in the community, the school's location, and the SES of households. In Ghana, as described in Chapter 3, school districts are not based on residential areas, and choosing schools is eminently possible. Thus, some guardians who have financial means and transportation can send their children to private schools in urban areas, even though they live in rural areas. Thus,

Table 5.5 Trend of school enrollment of case study schools and their surrounding public basic schools

	Year	2014	2015	2016	2017
	Education level				
School A	KG/Primary	213 (135)	230 (145)	220 (130)	160 (107)
Surrounding school 1	KG/Primary	143 (86)	203 (135)	140 (89)	163 (120)
Surrounding school 2	KG/Primary/ JHS	341 (189)	327 (175)	327 (181)	358 (241)
Surrounding school 3	KG/Primary/ JHS	327 (124)	310 (145)	320 (154)	303 (170)
Surrounding school 4	KG/Primary/ JHS	481 (242)	525 (265)	506 (249)	580 (278)
School B	KG/Primary	102 (73)	55 (35)	89 (45)	84 (47)
Surrounding school 5	KG/Primary	96 (56)	77 (56)	69 (50)	98 (62)
Surrounding school 6	KG/Primary	87 (56)	77 (48)	89 (61)	81 (60)
Surrounding school 7	KG/Primary/ JHS	225 (122)	214 (110)	237 (120)	245 (123)
Surrounding school 8	KG/Primary/ JHS	232 (121)	196 (105)	187 (106)	187 (99)

Source: Author based on data from the Akatsi South District Education Office

Note: Figures within parentheses mean the number of primary school enrollment. Surrounding school 4 represents that two primary schools feed pupils to one JHS, thus I present them as one school for clear comparison. I put surrounding schools 2, 3, 4 for School A as those where graduates from School A proceed based on interviews from headteacher and pupils.

school enrollment indicates that the schools have good reputation from guardians. In addition, the amount of the CG awarded to each school is calculated according to school enrollment. There are no standardized examinations or assessments for all the pupils at primary education in Ghana. Thus, school enrollment data were adopted because they allowed me to access the data via the district education office and to make objective comparisons between schools.

Both Schools A and B faced the challenge of low enrollment. If we compare Schools A and B with their neighboring schools, schools with JHS sections had higher enrollment in their primary sections than schools without JHS sections (Table 5.5). If there were large size of schools with JHS sections nearby, it became difficult for schools that have only up to the primary section to increase their enrollment. Therefore, it is important to sustain and increase enrollment even at a small scale. The trend of enrollment over the years shows that there is higher enrollment at KGs than in primary sections, and as grades go up at the primary level, enrollment declines. Those schools with JHS sections also show increased enrollment in their primary sections than those without JHS sections. On the other hand, schools that only featured up to primary sections have either flat or decreasing trend in enrollment.

Socioeconomic status   School A had lower proportion of school communities members who graduated from SHS and above than the district average. Schools C and D, however, had better or almost identical scores to the district average, in terms of their educational background. This implies that Schools C and D occupied better positions than School A in terms of their school communities' educational background, among rural schools. Both case study schools were in a worse condition than the district average, according to several SES indicators. This implies that these case study schools are typical rural schools, where the living conditions are not well endowed.

Collective participation   In general, School C experienced more collective participation than the district average. School D scored lower than the district average in all the indicators, implying that some problems were occurring at School D. School A has a relatively good collective participation, taking into consideration its size.

Relational Trust   Table 5.3 shows the details of the RT, collective participation, and SES of the case study schools. Among the case study schools, School D has a lower "Teacher-parent RT" than the district average. This implies that something was wrong with the teacher–parent relationship.

Table 5.6 Details of teaching force

	Education level			Teacher qualification		Educational background			
	KG	Prim	JHS	Qualified	Unqualified	B	D	CA	SHS
School A	2(2)	4(0)	-	5	1	2	3	-	1
School B	1(0)	3(2)	-	3	1	1	2	-	1
School C	2(2)	6(3)	5(1)	13	0	-	10	1	-
School D	4(3)	6(1)	7(0)	13	4	2	10	2	3

Source: Annual School Census on February 2017 and headteacher questionnaire

Note 1: Figures in the columns show the number of teachers.

Note 2: Number in the bracket means the number of female teachers at each education level.

Note 3: In educational background, B, D, CA, and SHS denote bachelor, diploma in education, certificate A, and SHS, respectively.

Table 5.7 Headteachers' background

	Sex	Age	Educational background	Years of working as a teacher	Years of working as a headteacher
School A	Male	48	Bachelor	19 years (since 1998)	Since 2017
School B	Female	45	Bachelor	20 years (since 1997)	Since 2012
School C	Male	53	Certificate A	31 years (since 1986)	Since 2013
School D	Male	43	Bachelor	18 years (since 1999)	Since 2014

Source: Based on interviews with headteachers and headteacher questionnaire

Note: Data as of September 2017

School A scored almost the same as the district average in each RT. School C has relatively better RT values, except for "Headteacher-teacher RT." School B has relatively good RT, except for "Teacher-parent RT," but this needs to be analyzed further through a more in-depth study.

Teaching force   Schools A and B have suffered from shortages of teacher. They did not have one teacher for one grade. Schools C and D had adequate numbers of teachers to teach all of the education levels. Certainly, they also had teachers with relevant qualifications and educational backgrounds (Table 5.6).

The backgrounds of the headteachers at the four case study schools are shown in Table 5.7.

Findings from case study schools in relation to learning outcomes

I conducted a case study of two schools by examining whether RT was realized in factors of school management, leading to achieving learning outcomes. This contributed to answering the following questions posed by the quantitative study: (1) why do schools with similar SES have different levels of attainment in terms of the BECE? and (2) how will "Teacher-parent RT" affect BECE in the process?

Schools C and D had both been high-performing schools in rural areas, up until 2013. However, since 2013, School D has experienced a sharp decline in terms of its BECE district ranking, unlike School C. BECE is one of the critical agenda items that is often discussed in SMC or PTA general and executive meetings. It is critical for JHS grade 3 pupils to have better BECE results to allow them to proceed to a prominent SHS, which would then likely allow more pupils to enter universities. The BECE also represents the only comparable data in the district to show the quality of schools. Thus, school communities always have strong interests in the BECE results and have associated it with efforts by headteacher and teachers.

RT in "Parent, School, Community Ties"

"Parent, School, Community Ties" is closely associated with collective participation and "School communities-school RT." It was found that there were differences between School C and D in their "Parent, School, Community Ties," as shown in the extent of collective participation of each school (Table 5.3). It is important to understand why there were such differences in this "Parent, School, Community Ties" factor between the two schools.

It should be noted that the extent of collective participation at School D was satisfactory in the past. One teacher at School D recalled the situation before 2013 as follows:

> In 2013/2014, community was very friendly and cooperating. When we call for PTA meetings, they come. We do get more than 100 parents. Positive things happened was that they started to renovate school building (corridor) . . . When I came to the school in 2013, I love it. There were extra classes, pupils' discipline was good, and the BECE was good.
> (D20170926TC)

However, the chieftaincy issue was provoked in the 2013/2014 academic year. The headteacher described the situation as follows:

> The chieftaincy issue was about the legitimacy of the paramount chief here. The school and teachers try to be neutral on this matter. But if you

work with PTA or SMC chairperson, people see it from the different angle that the school is sided with PTA or SMC chairperson.

(D20170926HT)

One teacher lamented the current situation as follows.

This time when we call for the meeting, only 30 parents come. Sometimes we use gong-gong (note: the traditional way of calling community people) to inform parents of the PTA meeting on the day when people do not go for farming or market. We set a day for the meeting, but they do not come. Chieftaincy issue caused the problem. Various villages are divided. The case went into the court, but cracks are still there. That was a beginning of our wars, the problems.

(D20170926TC)

One parent bitterly mentioned the issue as follows.

Chieftaincy dispute became topical issue over the past three years . . . PTA chairperson support the chief and parents do not come to meetings due to that . . . The issue is a headache for her. If town is divided, they cannot progress.

(D20170926PA)

Even though SMC/PTA executive members and headteacher/teachers expected community members and guardians to participate in general meetings, they did not feel obliged to attend the meetings because the school communities were divided, owing to the community dispute.

On the contrary, School C has been maintained a stable relationship with geographical communities. The geographical community established this school, and when a teacher shortage occurred, community members visited to the education offices to ask for the deployment of teachers to the school.

Parents described their aspirations toward this school as follows:

In the past, there are less education opportunities for girls as parents believe that girls end up with in the kitchen, now such recognition has changed. If you are farmers, you have to rely on the weather, but if you have education and have your jobs at government, you do not rely on the weather.

(C20170922PA)

Another parent also expressed their strong emphasis on education: "If somebody (role model) go through this school, you will be doctor, MPs, teachers. This expectation makes parents put value on education" (C20170922PA).

It implies that such a strong expectation for education was a motivating factor for parents and community members to support school development.

To put this expectation into practice, parents performed their obligation to support teachers. Parents referred to their support for teachers as follows: "Four teachers are resident in this community. Some stay at MP's house. Teachers have to pay electricity but not for water . . . Community members provide foods for teachers when harvest time" (C20170922PA).

Teachers responded to such expectations by performing their obligations as teachers. One teacher mentioned as follows: Teacher organized classes during vacation. Some teachers living in the community taught students (C20170922TC).

In summary, "School communities-school RT" was not being realized in "Parent, School, Community Ties" at School D because expectations were not being met with obligations within the school communities. However, at School C, the school communities expected schools to produce better educational outcomes for pupils, and so they were obliged to support them. Teachers also responded to such expectations by performing their obligations. Thus, at School C, "School communities-school RT" was realized in "Parent, School, Community Ties" based on the solid foundation of the geographical communities.

RT in "School Learning Climate"

"School Learning Climate" refers to the extent to which schools and classrooms are safe and orderly in terms of school infrastructure and school atmosphere. The decline in collective participation observed at School D owing to the community divide had several negative impacts on the "School Learning Climate." First, the geographical communities used to make contributions to a town development fund for school, which amounted to GHC 600–800 as a monthly base; however, they no longer pay funds. One SMC/PTA executive member said the following: "People regarded that a few people at the fund collection committee are spending the money without accountability" (D20170926PA). This prevented School D from continuing to renovate its JHS school, which is now in danger of collapse (Figures 5.8 and 5.9).

Second, those who were related to School D or the village expected school development and offered the following support: textbooks, uniforms, drums, scholarship, and cement for the school library. However, such expectations were not met with positive reactions from community members. The headteacher mentioned as follows:

> In 2014/2015, a renowned lawyer donated his English textbooks free of charge to the school but as he is a lawyer of one group, three parents

Figure 5.8 JHS block in danger of collapse due to lack of funds (School D). Photograph by the author.

Figure 5.9 JHS corridor buttressed with a temporal structure (School D). Photograph by the author.

told their kids to send back the books to school because they are from a different group within chieftaincy divide.

(D20170926HT)

Teachers also mentioned another case in which external support was not utilized as follows: "UK-based businessman from this village used to support the school but stopped around 2014 and a lawyer donated his English textbooks to the school but some guardians refused to accept for their children."

(D20170926TC)

The headteacher also raised the issue of the school library and stated as follows:

Member of Parliament donated 50 bags of cement for building school library. . . . After discussing the site for the library, the change of the site was suggested by other chief where school canteen is supposed to be built. Thus the library project stopped for two years now.

(D20170926HT)

School D, which has had a long history since its establishment in 1935, had various channels of external support for school development. However, this support was incapacitated and stopped being utilized owing to the community divide. In this sense, expectations from the school communities, including those who provide external support to the school, were not accompanied with obligations by those who were supposed to utilize such support.

On the other hand, School C improved its "School Learning Climate," which has been their challenges. Parents discussed in the PTA/SMC meeting and agreed that: "Water is their biggest problem. Children would have to obtain permission to go home to drink and after which they would not return to the school" (C20161111PA).

In the meeting minutes, the SMC chairperson said that numerous attempts have been made to bring water to the school (KG), but they had failed. They promised that they would make sure that water was brought to the KG. It was also mentioned that this water issue was becoming stagnated and that the PTA/SMC and the community must take steps to address the water problems with urgency (PTA general meeting minutes, C20161111). In the following year, it was recorded that the SMC chairperson was very happy to inform that water problem for the primary and JHS sections had been solved, leaving only the KG to be dealt with (PTA general meeting minutes, C20170724). It was confirmed by teachers that the headteacher had discussed with the PTA chairperson, and was able to bring pipe-borne water into the school compound (C20170922TC) (Figures 5.10 and 5.11). This implied that School C was able to address its long-standing challenge of the water issue, which affected pupils' school participation. In summary, while "School communities-school RT" is not realized in "School Learning Climate" at School D, it was realized in School C.

RT in "Pedagogical factors"

"Pedagogical Factors" is considered as the extent of "Time for Learning," "Supplementary Resources," and "Dynamics of Student Learning," composed of "Motivation" and "School Participation" (Bryk et al., 2010). As teachers and pupils are part of the instructional triangle which Bryk et al. (2010) articulated, I decomposed their motivation into "Teacher Motivation" and "Pupil Motivation."

School participation requires a basic level of parenting, such as providing breakfast before coming to schools. At School C, all the possible support for pupils to participate in school was emphasized by various stakeholders. The headteacher advised parents not to give pupils other responsibilities during school hours, as well as not to give pupils house chores, because this would take attention away from their study.

Figure 5.10 School building (School C). Photograph by the author.

Figure 5.11 Piped water facility (School C). Photograph by the author.

The interviewed pupils confirmed that their guardians provided support for their school participation as follows: "Parents make me come to school on time and without absence . . ..Parents do not force pupils to do house chores and let me do homework. Parents ask whether I finish homework" (C20170922PU).

While teachers mentioned that they expected guardians to provide breakfast for children, guardians also agreed that it was their responsibility to provide uniforms, breakfast, money for lunch, and exercise books. According to pupils, their parents have provided breakfast, money for lunch, pencils, erasers, and exercise books. If they run out of materials needed for school, guardians will provide them for pupils (C20170922PU). Such pupils' comments explained that guardians responded to the headteacher and teachers' calls for supporting pupils' school participation to some extent.

On the other hand, the headteacher at School D recalled his pupils' school participation in the 2014/2015 academic year as follows:

> The JHS Grade three pupils were stubborn; they destroyed academic performance, they did not stay in the classroom, they did not do homework, and often after the first break, they go out from the school. Sometimes teachers had to chase them at their various houses to come back to school.
>
> (D20170926HT)

As such, pupils' school participation with support from guardians generated differences between the two schools.

Securing time for learning in the form of extra classes or classes during the vacations is critical. Parents referred to teachers in terms of their good performance at School C and supported teachers: We are proud of teachers. Pupils' performance is improving. This is thanks to teachers . . . When parents asked teachers to do extra classes without pay, teachers do respond (C20170922PA).

Teachers also mentioned that they were able to improve learning outcomes, as part of their responsibility to respond to the expectations of parents and community members:

> Hard working. Teachers organize class during vacation. Some teacher living in the community teach students. When one teacher was on further study, he gave his contact number to students and if they have any problems, they can call to the teachers. Not every students do but some did.
>
> (C20170922TC)

Regarding the organization of extra classes for the BECE, there was intense debate within the school communities at School C. The headteacher mentioned that they understood that some parents were calling for extra classes, but that unfortunately the government has warned against the organization of extra classes. The headteacher, therefore, did not want to risk organizing extra classes. However, suggestions were made by guardians that the PTA should write to the office (GES) to obtain permission to organize extra classes (SMC/PTA general meeting minutes, C20161111). From the interviews and meeting minutes, it was not clear whether any extra classes took place as a result. However, this shows how guardians and community members were committed to organizing extra classes despite the cancellation policy by the district education office.

On the contrary, the decline in resource mobilization for school development affected "Pedagogical factors" to a large extent at School D. One teacher referred to the reduced learning time as follows: "Extra classes had been conducted throughout Primary Grade one to JHS Grade three. However, they stopped in 2014/2015 academic year and parents are no longer paying" (D20170926TC).

The headteacher also mentioned that even though parents expected that extra classes should be organized and had agreed to pay for them, they did not perform their obligations to pay for them.

> In October 2017, at the PTA meeting, it was agreed that the school should have extra classes for Form 2 and 3 (expected fee is GHC1.2 for 5 days), but only a handful people paid for it.
>
> (D20180920HT)

School D has suffered from delayed CGs and lack of resource mobilization by school communities, which has affected supplementary resources for pedagogy in classrooms. One teacher described the serious lack of teaching and learning materials as follows: "Last two years we do not have money for buying chalks. Using the internally generated fund (selling crafts) for buying the chalks. CG comes but delayed. 2016/2017 2nd and 3rd tranche have arrived just now" (D20170926TC).

The division within the geographical and school communities surrounding School D also affected teachers' motivation, which is part of the pedagogical factor. The headteacher described teachers' feelings as follows: "With this issue, most of teachers have opted for transfer as they think that all the endeavors go in vain. Teachers say that community members are reluctant" (D20170926HT).

The headteacher also had strong patience, even though the chieftaincy issue had seriously affected their school. He stressed the followings:

> As a head, I tell teachers that they should look at their inner, and intrinsic motivation. With that, most of us can stay on. You are posted to a school not to a community so it is for you to bring changes. Let us do our part.
>
> (D20170926HT)

However, the teachers did not share in the same patience with their headteacher. When extra classes with pay did not materialize, owing to lack of guardians' contributions, the headteacher asked teachers to cooperate with morning classes without pay. However, teachers insisted the followings: "Until (behavioral) changes happen in pupils, we do not organize morning classes" (D20180920TC).

While the headteacher aimed to improve the BECE results by way of organizing morning classes, teachers could not agree to such strategies without pupils' commitment to learning and parent/guardians' obligations to provide basic support for pupils. Despite expectations from the headteacher about cooperation for morning classes, teachers did not able to feel obliged to respond to such expectations owing to the lack of pupils' commitments to learning, and their lack of respect for teachers. In that sense, "Headteacher-teacher RT" is not realized in "Teachers' motivation" and "Learning time" to prepare for the BECE.

"Pupil's motivation" to learn is also critical to their learning. Pupils at School C showed their high motivations influenced by their teachers and their expectations for the future. They said that teachers were hardworking because students passed the BECE well, they did not joke around, they were serious, and they provided homework for every subject. Pupils also referred to their motivation to learn with the expectations for their future. One pupil mentioned this as follows: "To proceed to SHS, pupils do homework, review what they have learned in the day by going through their exercise books" (C20170922PU).

With such pupils' motivation, teachers were highly motivated at School C. Teachers said how they enhanced pupils' learning and motivation as follows: "Teachers motivate and encourage pupils using teachers as an example" (C20170922TC).

Guardians acknowledged teachers' efforts by referring that they were proud of their teachers, because pupils' performance was improving. This was to show gratitude to the teachers. Guardians helped teachers who resided in the geographical communities with water issues. It appears that guardians wanted to support teachers in return for what teachers had done for pupils' learning.

On the other hand, at School D, pupils did not show their motivation to learn, nor did they respond to their teachers' expectations. Though teachers organized morning classes for JHS grade 3, the attendance was not as expected. Teachers and guardians held the common view that pupils were not motivated to learn. One teacher lamented over this situation as follows: "Pupils do not see the necessity to learn. Some of them have textbooks but they are not serious about education, they watch TV at home without study" (D20170926TC).

Lack of pupils' discipline has become a critical issue at School D. This has included a lack of respect for guardians and teachers, not doing the expected homework, watching TV at night without doing homework, and going out for wake-keeping (dancing with music at funerals) at weekends. One guardian mentioned how the lack of pupils' discipline affected teaching and learning (teachers): "The teachers are willing to teach but pupils are not willing to learn. The headteacher called parents and complained about discipline of pupils. Guardians talked to pupils but they do not obey" (D20180920PA).

Teachers saw that the lack of pupils' discipline came from guardians, because they were not encouraging their wards to study at home and talk negatively about the teachers. This low pupils' motivation, caused by a lack of guardians' support, made teachers lose their motivations to commit themselves to teaching. One teacher bitterly mentioned this as follows: "If children are serious about picking up learning, it motivates teachers to do more . . . Without discipline, nothing is helpful" (D20170926TC).

In summary, School C was able to sustain its learning outcomes, with RT being realized in each of the factors of school management.

It had a solid foundation due to stable support from its geographical and school communities and was well equipped in a professional capacity. Water issues had been addressed, in consultation between the head-teacher and the SMC chairperson, which would contribute to pupils' school participation. Efforts to secure learning opportunities have been made because the school communities opposed the cancellation of extra classes for BECE, teachers were committed to their work, and pupils were motivated to learn with support from their parents and teachers. This could explain how RT is realized in the factors of school management, and how this has led to sustained learning outcomes at School C (Figure 5.12).

On the other hand, in the case of School D, there was declining collective participation, owing to the community divide. This seriously affected RT in other factors. Support for this school in terms of the "School Leaning Climate," has been incapacitated due to the community divide. The lack of teachers' motivation mirrored that of pupils' motivation and of guardians' support for pupils. As teachers and pupils are two important subjects in the instructional triangle developed by Bryk et al. (2010), this affected the "Pedagogical factors" to a large extent. Despite well-equipped "Professional Capacity," the declining collective participation, owing to the community divide, hindered external support and school learning climate, including both teachers' and pupils' motivation. This could explain why School D's BECE ranking has declined to the bottom of the district within a short period of time (Figure 5.13).

Finally, by comparing Schools C and D, I would like to answer the following questions posed in the quantitative study: (1) why do schools with similar SES have different levels of attainment in terms of the BECE? and (2) how does "Teacher-parent RT" affect the BECE?

First, though SES and the extent of "Professional Capacity" factor are similar, the "Parent, School, Community ties" factor was different, shown in the extent of collective participation. Such differences in collective participation affected the two schools in terms of their "Time for learning," in the form of extra classes, and "Supplementary resources" needed for learning in "Pedagogical factors." "Teacher-parent RT" affected the BECE because it is the results of pupils' school participation, pupils' motivation, guardians' support, and teachers' motivation. The difference between Schools C and School D in "Teacher-parent RT" explains the differences of pupils' school participation, pupils' motivation, guardians' support, and teachers' motivation in "Pedagogical factors," which lead to the BECE result.

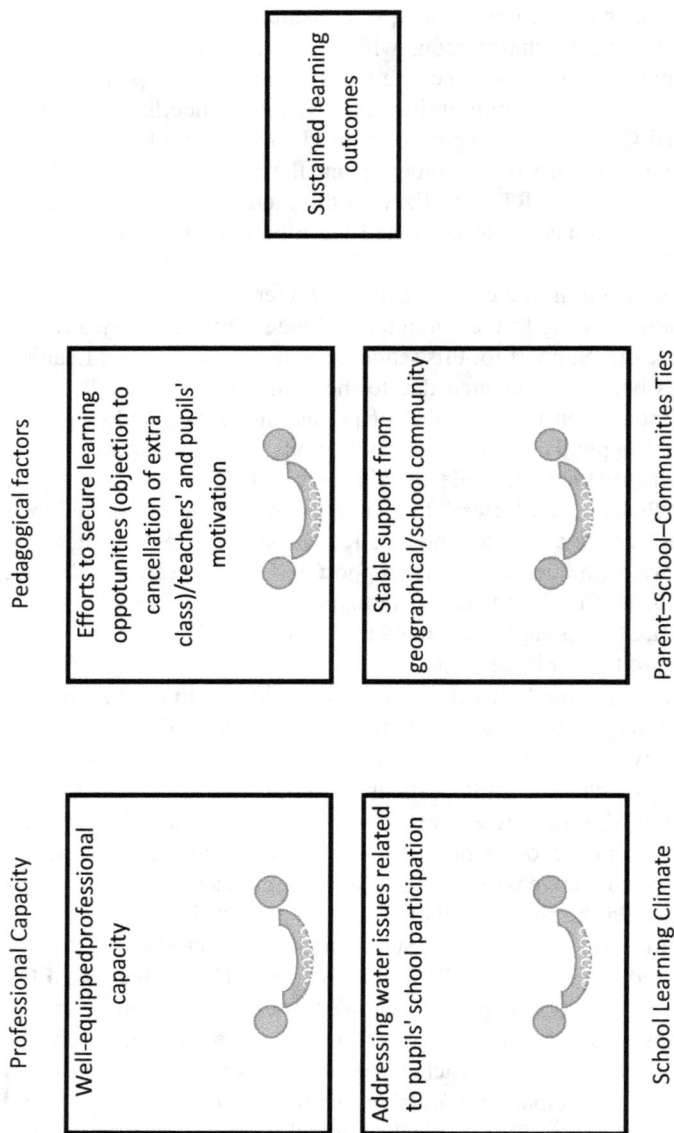

Figure 5.12 Structure of how relationships between actors and factors in school management lead to sustained learning outcomes (School C).

Source: developed by the author.

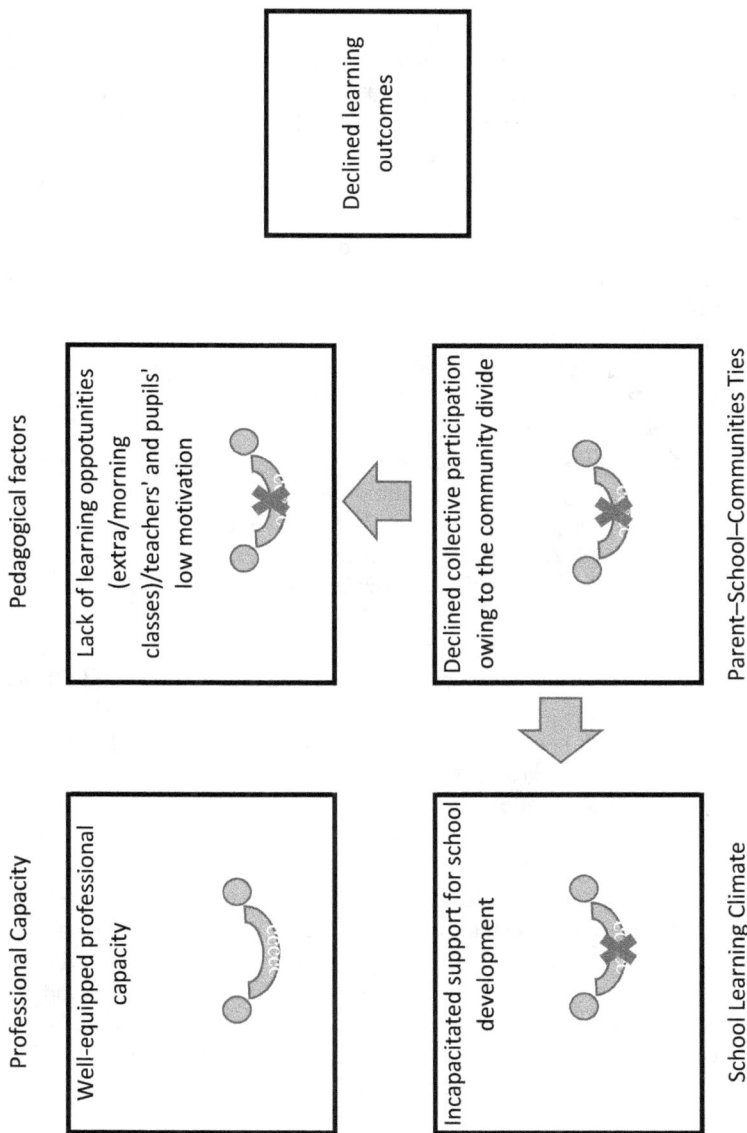

Figure 5.13 Structure of how relationships between actors and factors in school management lead to declined learning outcomes (School D). Developed by the author.

Findings from case study schools in relation to school enrollment

I conducted a case study of two schools through examining whether RT was realized in factors of school management to sustain school enrollment. This contributed to revealing the following question, raised by the quantitative study: why is it true that the higher extent of collective participation schools have, the larger enrollment they have, especially in rural areas? A further question is how does higher "School communities-school RT" in schools affect the extent of collective participation?

As discussed in the previous part of the book, public basic schools without JHS sections have suffered from low school enrollment. Both Schools A and B have suffered from low school enrollment. However, there have been differences in sustaining school enrollment between the two schools.

While School A has sustained its enrollment over time, school enrollment at School B has stagnated. Owing to competition among schools based on parents' desire to choose better learning environments, it was difficult for schools to sustain school enrollment that they were expected to receive from their surrounding geographical communities.

As shown in Table 5.5, school enrollment at School A had been stable at around 210 to 220 but had declined to 160 in 2017. In the CTA (Community-Teachers-Association) general meetings, the school communities were worried about the decreasing trend in school enrollment (February 28, 2017; May 30, 2017). Parents, pupils, and teachers had unanimous views about decreasing school enrollment at grade 6. The parents lamented this as follows: P6 enrollment is not encouraging (at this moment 11). Attrition rate from P6 to JHS form 1 is high. As there are no JHS attached to the school, those who go to JHS have to go to ***, ***, and *** (A20170925PA).

Thus, it is a critical challenge for School A to sustain school enrollment because neighboring basic schools with JHS sections can attract pupils at the primary level.

According to the photo records taken by the headteacher, the school enrollment written on the blackboard at the headteacher office was 163 in April 2017, when the headteacher was appointed to this school. In the record by the headteacher in July 2018, school enrollment was 173. It should be noted that the enrollment figures vary depending on timing of data collection. However, while surrounding schools with JHS sections increased their enrollment, a little increase in school enrollment at School A showed a positive sign for school improvement.

On the contrary, school enrollment at School B fell to 55 in 2015 and has not since recovered to its level of 2014. When I conducted the field visit at School B, there were only three classrooms, in addition to the headteacher's office. They conducted multigrade teaching, owing to the limited number of pupils (see Figure 5.22).

RT in "Professional Capacity"

According to parents, School A suffered from a teacher shortage. In fact, School A had only six teachers, including the headteacher, and the head-teacher had to teach grade 2. Grade 5 and grade 6, as well as grade 3 and 4, were combined into one class, respectively, owing to the teacher shortage. The headteacher also had to teach Grade 4 by himself. As a measure to address this challenge, the headteacher planned to receive mentees, namely, student teachers from the nearby Akatsi College of Education.

In Ghana, student teachers are deployed to schools and then conduct their teaching practice for the whole year. Schools receiving mentees should meet conditions such as providing free accommodation nearby schools and this requires support from both parents and community members. According to the records of the Akatsi College of Education, only 27 among 86 public basic schools in the district received student teachers in 2017/2018 academic year. This means that not many schools were able to meet such conditions. To respond to the headteacher's expectations, the school communities performed their obligations to provide free accommodations to student teachers, resulting in School A receiving six student teachers in the academic year 2017/2018. The objective of receiving student teachers was not to provide alternative labor forces for the receiving schools but to train and supervise them on the field. However, receiving student teachers made a difference to School A, which was suffering from a teacher shortage. The headteacher mentioned this as follows: "Student teachers bring effects, they teach Grade four with two persons, which I am teaching currently. We sit down and advise student teachers" (A20180924HT).

The school communities performed their obligations to respond to the headteacher's expectations. This in turn lead to the school receiving student teachers, which acted as precious human resources for School A, as they contributed to addressing the teacher shortage. As two student teachers were engaged in Grade 4, the headteacher no longer needed to teach Grade 4 and could then concentrate on his administrative duty and supervising role for the student teachers. As such, "School communities-school RT" was realized in "Professional Capacity," to provide a better environment to enable teachers to perform their professional capacity, owing to the collective participation from the school communities.

"Headteacher-teacher RT" was also realized in "Professional Capacity" at School A. Owing to the previous headteacher's frequent absence, teachers at School A tended to finish lessons by either 12 am or 1 pm, instead of 2 pm, which is an official closing time. The current headteacher aimed to engender changes of teachers by acting as a role model to them. It is important for a headteacher that pupils come to school early, and that teachers and guardians perform their expected duties. Teachers, guardians, and pupils had a good impression about this headteacher's commitment, which represented a sharp contrast with the previous headteacher. The teachers mentioned this as follows: "The previous headteachers did not come to school while teachers came to school without problems. The current head is more time conscious."

The headteacher used the strategy to change the school by making teachers being time conscious and ready for instructional activities. Although the headteacher lived outside of the geographical communities where the school was located, he came early to the school, vetted teachers' lesson notes (Figure 5.14), checked the submission of lesson notes by teachers (Figure 5.15), and recorded the arrival times for all the teachers (Figure 5.16).

Pupils also described the headteacher's behavior as follows: "The headteacher work hard compared to the previous head. He is at school by 7 am. He is the first teacher to come to school and he comes to school every day. The previous head did not come to school regularly."

The SMC executive members also echoed what the teachers and pupils said, stating that the headteacher brought positive changes to make teachers

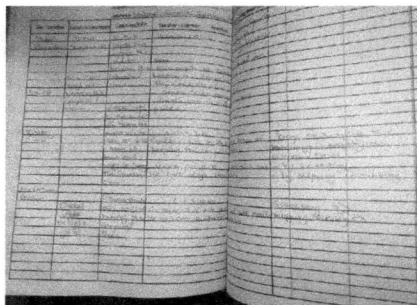

Figure 5.14 A lesson note vetted by the headteacher. Photograph by the author.

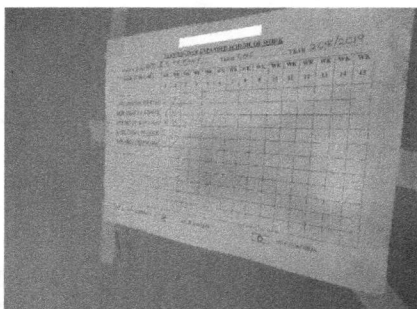

Figure 5.15 A checklist for submission of expanded scheme works (lesson notes). Photograph by the author.

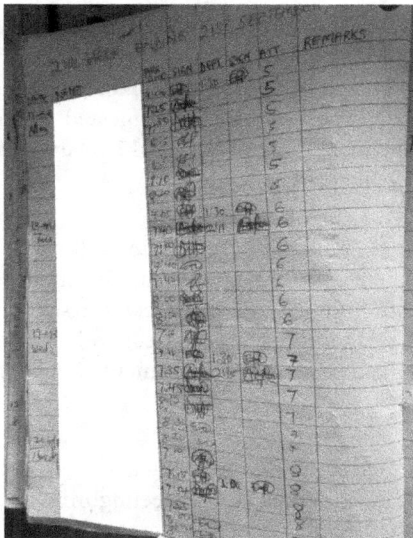

Figure 5.16 A checklist of weekly teacher attendance. Photograph by the author.

come to school before classes start around 8 am and to close at the official closing time at 2 pm.

If teachers come to school, deliver lessons, and work until the official closing time, such teachers' commitment as human resources can be effectively utilized. Thus, teachers responded to the headteacher's expectations by changing their working behavior and performed their expected obligations as teachers.

School B also suffered from a teacher shortage. According to the headteacher, the following events showed lack of collective participation hindered "Professional capacity" (B20170201HT). First, the school communities could not provide or rent accommodation for teachers within the geographical communities near School B. One transferred teacher requested to stay within the geographical communities, but this was not possible owing to lack of accommodation. Second, School B could not receive mentees from the Akatsi College of Education because the school communities could not provide free accommodation. Third, the teachers expected to participate in fee-paying workshops organized by the Ghana Association of Science Teachers (GAST). However, their expectations were not met with obligations by the headteachers. This was because the headteacher could not obtain adequate funds to sponsor their fees and transportation.

RT in "Parent, School, Community Ties"

"Parent, School, Community Ties" includes both collective participation as members of school communities and individual participation as individual parents. School A was able to enrich its school finance by increasing the amount of PTA funds. The headteacher suggested collecting GHC 2 per pupil, at the PTA general meeting in May 2017. They mentioned the necessity of increased PTA funds as follows:

> Besides capitation grant and PTA's payment for KG attendant, I asked parents to pay GHC 2 per child per term. This money is used for maintenance of school building and pad locks for schools door to prevent pupils from entering after school. As capitation grant comes late and not enough, this is a necessary arrangement at this moment.
>
> (A20170925HT)

As a result, it was agreed at the CTA meeting that this increase in the amount of PTA funds would be accepted (CTA meeting minutes, A20180928). To respond to headteacher's expectation for increased PTA funds and decision-making at the CTA meeting, it was confirmed in the headteacher's interview that GHC 496 has been collected in the academic year 2017/2018, which was far more than GHC 133.33, the average amount of mobilized PTA funds from 2014 to 2016 (A20180919HT). This shows that RT was realized between the school communities and the school in terms of the "Parent, School, Community Ties."

On the contrary, School communities–school RT was not realized in "Parent, School, Community ties" at School B. The historical background between its two geographical communities has prevented School B from sustaining school enrollment and collective participation. The headteacher explained this background as follows:

> The participation of parents at the PTA general meeting is low. If the total number of parents is 100, the number of participants is around 15. Not all the SMC/PTA executive members come to the meetings. Owing to dispute over the location of School B, some guardians decided not to send their children to School B and more than 30 pupil moved to other school. Parents and community members agreed but could not implement.
>
> (B20170201HT)

Even though the teachers highlighted the need to retain enrollment, parents could not meet such expectations due to the lack of collective participation. The lack of RT in "Parent, School, Community Ties" affected its "School

Learning Climate," "Professional Capacity," and "Pedagogical Factors." More details are provided in the following sections.

RT in "School Learning Climate"

"School Learning Climate" is regarded as the extent to which schools and classrooms are ready for teaching and learning, in terms of school infrastructure. School A enhanced its school learning climate as school facilities and its related programs (Figures 5.17 and 18). The possibility of introducing a school feeding program and the necessity of constructing a JHS were discussed as methods to increase enrollment, and decisions were made to take necessary actions to realize these programs. The headteacher mentioned that if the school were to start a school feeding program, this would be attractive for children, and higher enrollment would be expected. The headteacher stated their expectations regarding the school feeding program as follows:

> Sometimes pupils do not have concentration because they do not have breakfast. A unit committee member, who is a member of the New Patriotic Party (NPP) have discussed this issue with their stakeholders. With school feeding program, the school can attract more pupils. Some pupils who are residing in this community go to *** because of school feeding program. Pupils like foods.
>
> (A20180919HT)

The circuit supervisor in charge of this school pleaded with the assembly members to ensure that the school feeding program would be introduced to the school, to enable children to stay in school. Parents also mentioned that the unit committee representative was trying hard to bring the school feeding program to this school. The unit committee member promised that by the end of the year, the school feeding program would be in this school.

In terms of the JHS facilities, the community members and parents expressed their desire to establish a JHS. To respond to such expectations, the headteacher felt obliged to write letters to the District Chief Executive and the District Director of Education to establish a JHS in this community. The headteacher said that if they were to have a JHS here, those who were sending their children to nearby schools might come back to this school, meaning that school enrollment would increase. To construct a JHS section at School A, an adequate enrollment for Primary grade 6 is necessary. At the same time, having a JHS will be attractive for parents to send their children to School A.

The introduction of a school feeding program and the construction of a JHS were extremely selective, owing to limited budget of School A and the

Figure 5.17 Outlook of school building (School A). Photograph by the author.

Figure 5.18 Church building under construction (next to school building) (School A). Photograph by the author.

district overall. They may depend on political decisions regarding whether the school communities belong to the constituencies of the District Chief Executive. As it takes some time for these programs to be executed, a follow-up investigation is needed to track the progress of these programs continuously. These narratives show that School A put the expectations and decisions made by the school communities into practice, by way of utilizing the influence of the unit committee representative member or the assembly members.

Improving the school learning climate would be attractive for both pupils and teachers. School A discussed that they had difficulties in implementing Information, Communication, and Technology (ICT) classes without computers at the school. To respond to such demands, the headteacher and teachers discussed purchasing a computer. They planned in their action plan to have ICT classes four times in the first term starting in September 2017. It was planned that the Japan Oversees Cooperation Volunteer, who was dispatched to the Akatsi South district education office, would go around schools in the district and instruct pupils how to use keyboards. After consultations between the headteacher and teachers, it was reported at the CTA meeting that School A had purchased a laptop computer using the CG (Figure 5.20). The ICT classes were implemented as planned (Figure 5.19), and pupils had opportunities to learn how to use computers. This enabled the teachers who had wished to purchase computers to implement ICT classes.

On the other hand, the low extent of collective participation had affected the "School Learning Climate." According to the headteacher, health facilities were lacking, such as veronica buckets, pipe-born water, and classrooms (B20170201HT).

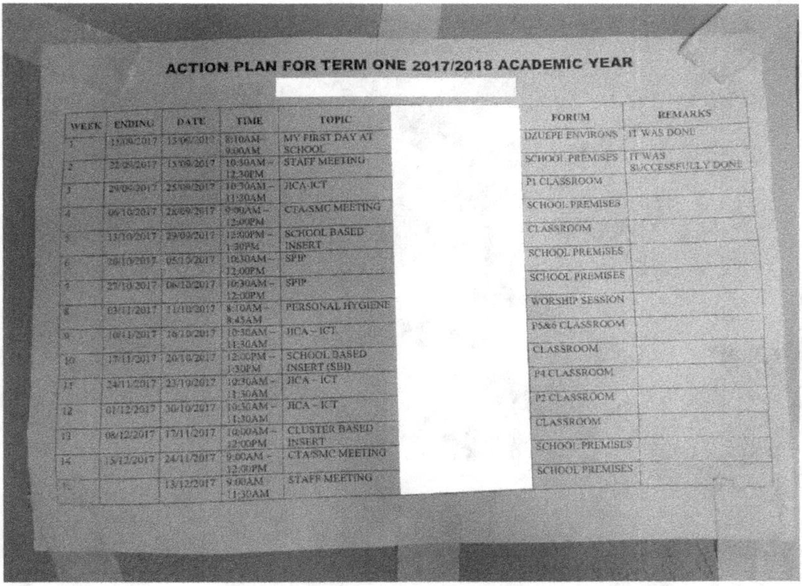

Figure 5.19 ICT lessons planned in the action plan in 2017/2018 (School A). Photograph by the author.

In addition, the headteacher proposed that classrooms for KG should be constructed to avoid the primary classrooms being used as temporary measures. KG classrooms were to be constructed in other geographical community, whereas School B is located at the other geographical community. Thus, the SMC chairperson expressed their expectation that the two geographical communities should reconcile. It was agreed that KG classrooms should be constructed (PTA general meeting, B20120517). However, it was discussed that the KG classrooms should not be built away from the primary classrooms – they should be attached. As a result, the two geographical communities could not reach consensus. Thus, a "seven-person committee" was established to discuss this issue with the chiefs and the elders (PTA general meeting, B20140212). However, the issue of KG classrooms was mentioned on the agenda, but there was no report from the seven-person committee (PTA general meeting, B20151013). Finally, it was proposed by the SMC chairperson that the school communities needed to rely on external support such as NGOs to construct KG classrooms.

Figure 5.20 A purchased laptop computer (School A). Photograph by the author.

Moreover, it was agreed that a KG attendant should be recruited, and the school communities mobilized 50 GHC in total, namely, 50 peswas per pupil for the KG attendant's salary (PTA general meeting, B20140212). It was discussed again that this contribution must be mobilized to pay for a KG attendant (PTA general meeting, B20151013). However, according to the headteacher, the extent of collective participation remained low; thus, the school communities could not pay for the KG attendant salary and the efforts to recruit a KG attendant have been suspended (B20170201HT) (Figures 5.21 and 5.22).

RT in "Pedagogical factors"

"Pedagogical Factors" is considered as the extent of "Time for Learning," "Supplementary Resources," and "Dynamics of Student Learning," composed of "Motivation" and "School Participation." As teachers and pupils are part of the instructional triangle, I decomposed motivation into "Teacher Motivation" ' and "Pupil Motivation." Upon his appointment to the school in March 2017, the headteacher initiated a pedagogical activity in order to improve pupils' school participation. Pupils from Grade one to six were

Figure 5.21 Outlook of school building (School B). Photograph by the author.

Figure 5.22 KG pupils mixed up in a primary class (School B). Photograph by the author.

divided into three groups, using the colors of red, green, and yellow. Pupils in different colored groups competed for marks by coming to school early, fetching water for handmade tippy taps (Figure 5.23), cleaning the school compound, and getting dressed neatly. The results of their marks were written on the blackboard (Figure 5.24) and the best group was praised every Friday. They received some prizes, such as biscuits and drinks, at the end of each term. The headteacher consulted with teachers in terms of this activity, and teachers agreed to support it. For instance, the teachers agreed to implement this activity and supported efforts to raise some money for buying prizes. Teachers mentioned that this initiative was effective in its initial stage, but its effects have faded over time. Therefore, they need to restart the initiative to avoid pupils' lateness in the new academic year, by providing more ideas from teachers.

The case study showed that pupils had high motivation owing to the new initiative of the headteacher. The interviewed pupils made the following positive remarks about the pedagogical activities at School A: "Because pupils' discipline was good, pupils were attentive to teachers and the teachers and student teachers were actively engaged with teaching pupils." Pupils mentioned that they needed to go to school, do homework, and read books if they wanted to proceed to a higher level of education or to get their jobs in the future. Pupils were also in favor of the headteacher's initiative to introduce a computer to the school. This implies that pupils who may not have access to computers at home wanted to learn how to use a computer at this school before proceeding to the nearby JHS, because they knew that there were computers for pupils to use. The headteacher's leadership affected pupils' motivation for learning, which was crucial for them to continue their enrollment at the primary school and proceed to JHS.

On the contrary, it was discussed at School B that parents requested teachers to provide evening classes for pupils and supervise them during the classes. However, because teachers did not reside near the school, the headteacher objected to the request, and as a result, pedagogical activities by teachers did not occur in response to the expectations of guardians (PTA general meeting minutes, B20120517).

The declining school enrollment was a demotivating factor for teachers. The headteacher mentioned that the current enrollment is 87, which was not encouraging for teachers (B20170201HT). Generally speaking in Ghana, parents are more likely to send their children to schools with low teacher-pupil ratios, because they do not want overcrowded classrooms (World Bank, 2003). However, field observations and Figures 5.25 and 5.26 both showed that the number of pupils was far less than the expected one and that lessons were not active due to the limited number of pupils.

Figure 5.23 Hand-made tippy tap (School A). Photograph by the author.

In summary, the headteacher started his initiative to attract more pupils to School A and the school communities were able to respond to this initiative by meeting and mobilizing resources for school development in the "Parent, School, Community Ties" factor (Figure 5.27). In the "Professional

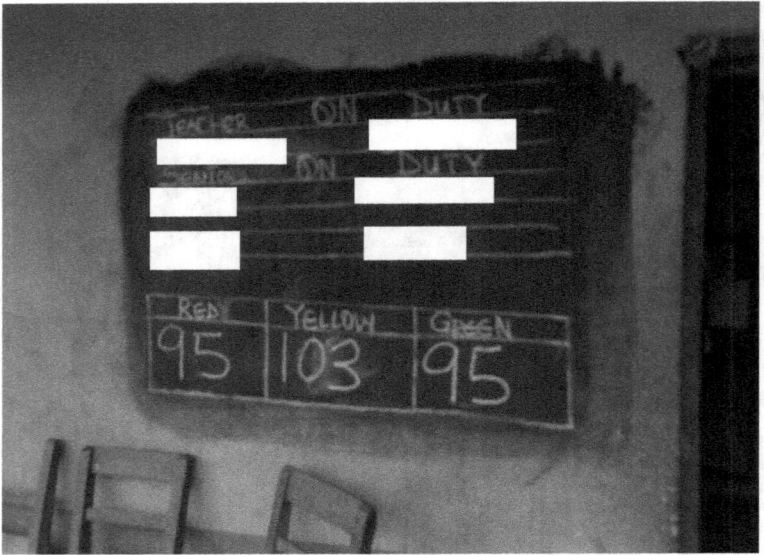

Figure 5.24 Blackboard on the corridor, which shows scores of three groups (red, yellow, and green) (School A). Photograph by the author.

Figure 5.25 Lesson with low teacher–pupil ratio (School B). Photograph by the author.

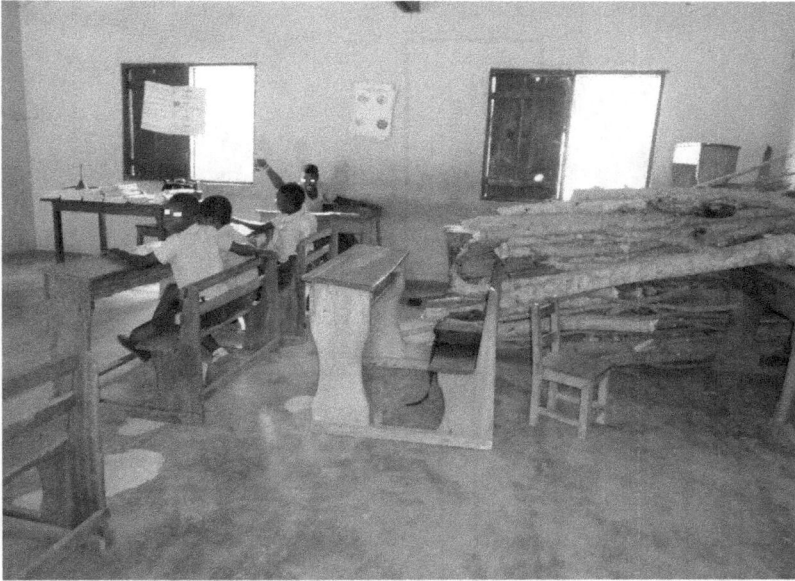

Figure 5.26 Classroom occupied with a few pupils and lots of timbers (School B). Photograph by the author.

Capacity" factor, the school communities also responded to the headteacher's expectation to receive mentees by providing free accommodations while teachers became committed to their work due to the headteacher's working attitude. This contributed to securing time for learning, which affected "Pedagogical factors." The school feeding program, the construction of a JHS, and the purchase of a laptop computer in "School Learning Climate" were also meant to entice pupils from other schools. The headteacher initiated pedagogical activities to let pupils attend school with pleasure, come on time without absence, and engage with ICT. This in turn motivated pupils to learn more. The realization of RT and connections between factors contributed to sustained school enrollment.

I wondered why sustained school enrollment was so important for the school communities at School A. Parents had their own individual desires for their children to succeed in their life through education:

> We want to our children to progress in their life. Even if they become farmers, they can make agriculture more modernized through education . . . We want our kids to be teachers, nurses, or somebody responsible in the society, and any government job.

(A20180919PA)

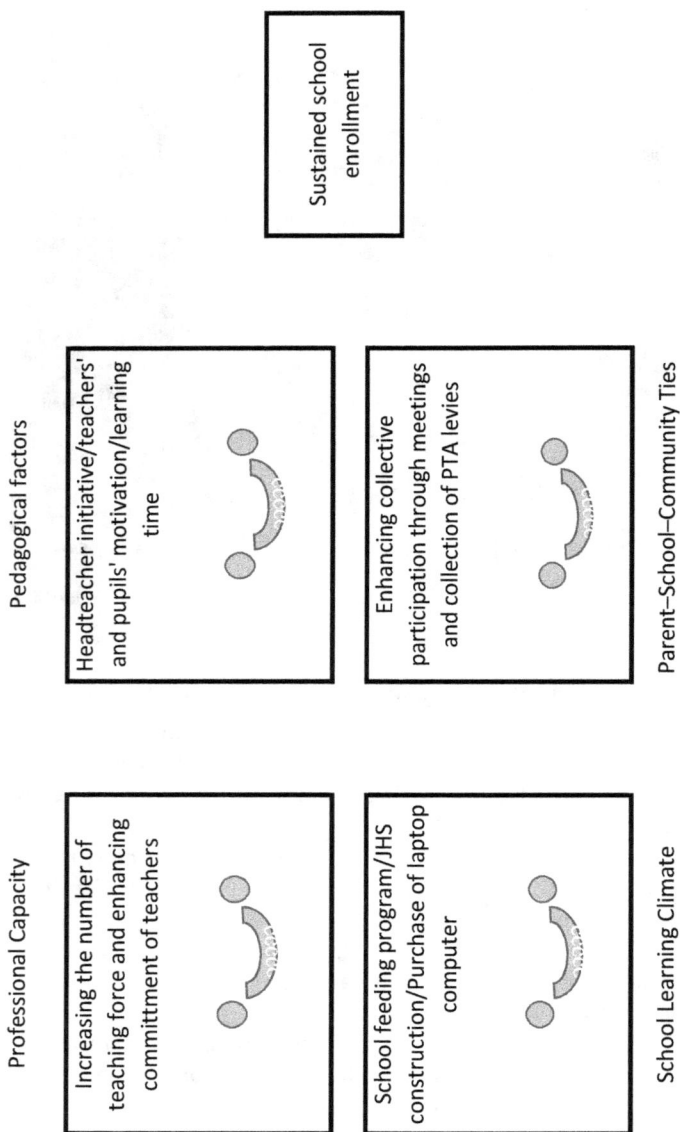

Figure 5.27 Structure of how relationships between actors and factors in school management lead to sustained school enrollment (School A). Developed by the author.

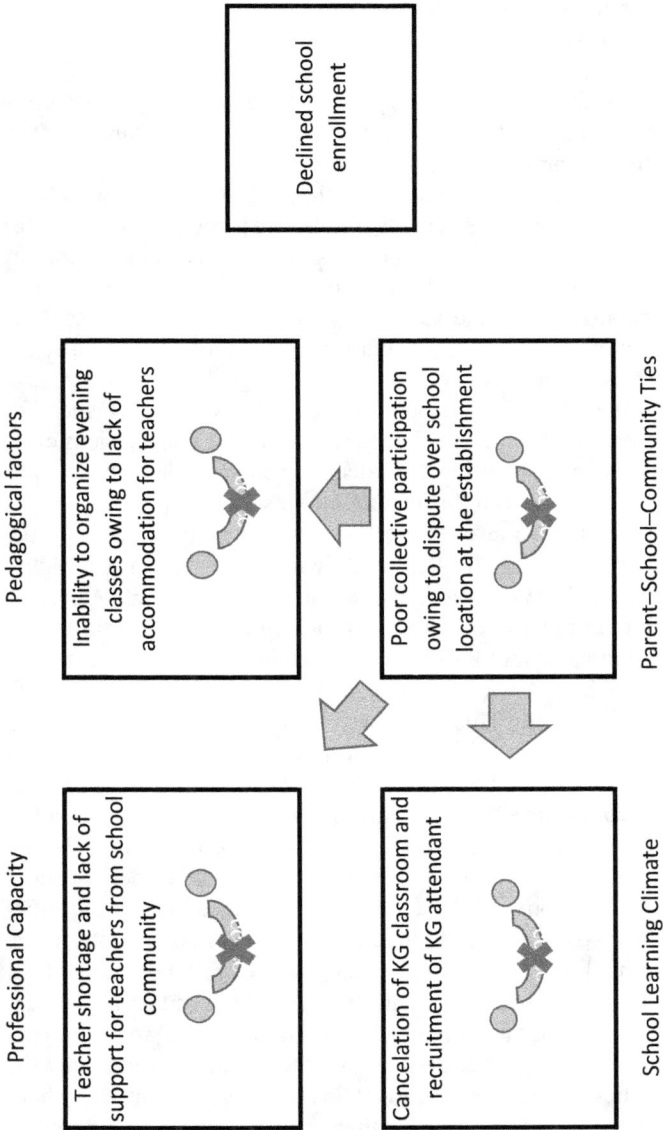

Professional Capacity

Pedagogical factors

Teacher shortage and lack of support for teachers from school community

Inability to organize evening classes owing to lack of accommodation for teachers

Cancelation of KG classroom and recruitment of KG attendant

Poor collective participation owing to dispute over school location at the establishment

Declined school enrollment

School Learning Climate

Parent–School–Community Ties

Figure 5.28 Structure of how relationships between actors and factors in school management lead to decline school enrollment (School B). Developed by the author.

One of the school community members expressed their collective participation as to why they placed value on education, as follows: "School belongs to this community. Products (pupils) will be good materials to community" (A20180919PA).

This showed that the education for children was designed to create a future for their children, as well as for the community. Thus, it was critical for parents and the school communities to sustain school enrollment to provide a conducive learning environment for children.

On the other hand, School B could not realize RT in the "Parent, School, Community Ties" factor owing to the lack of collective participation, which was rooted in the dispute over the school's locations, which had continued since its establishment. The low extent of collective participation hindered other factors and made RT unrealized. Thus, the teacher shortage has not been addressed, due to a lack of support from the school communities in the "Professional Capacity" factor; evening classes for pupils' learning were not organized in "Pedagogical factors." Furthermore, the KG classroom was not constructed and payment for a KG attendant was not done. The failure to realize RT became a vicious cycle of school management, where the low extent of collective participation was accompanied by low school enrollment and vice versa (Figure 5.28).

Finally, I would like to answer the following questions raised by the quantitative study: (1) Why did School A, with less SES, have a higher school enrollment? (2) Why was it that the higher the collective participation is, the higher school enrollment becomes? (3) How did higher "School communities-school RT" affect the extent of collective participation in schools? School A was located above the correlation line between SES and school enrollment. This means that School A had relatively higher enrollment, despite its low SES. This implies that collectives of school communities and its fragile households (as its constituents) – which both had lower SES, could sustain school enrollment by working collectively.

Comparing School A with School B, the realization of "School communities-school RT" determined the extent of collective participation. Stakeholders at School A believed that the school belonged to them and anticipated that pupils would be a good investment for their community. Thus, they expected schools to do something and felt obliged to support the school when the headteacher expected it from them. On the other hand, stakeholders at School B regarded that the school had been divided owing to the dispute over the school's location. Thus, even though the headteacher expected the school communities to do something to retain school enrollment, the school communities agreed to do something but then could not put that into practice.

Moreover, because collective participation was available at School A, it affected other factors in school management, which were geared toward sustaining school enrollment, triggered by the headteacher's initiative. On the contrary, the lack of collective participation at School B hindered other factors in school management, which created a vicious cycle between collective participation and school enrollment. This illustrates how collective participation can or cannot lead to school enrollment.

Findings from case study schools coping with pupils' discipline as a critical challenge

As stated previously, pupils' indiscipline has become a major concern for guardians in Ghana. It is difficult to quantify the extent of pupils' indiscipline, unlike the BECE results and school enrollment. However, pupils' indiscipline was a symbolic phenomenon, which can influence learning outcomes (owing to lack of pupils' motivation to learn), and school enrollment (owing to lack of pupils' willingness for school participation). Thus, it is significant to identify how school communities, guardians, and teachers can address pupils' indiscipline through the realization of RT.

Pupils' indiscipline, as exhibited in this case study, includes the following: lack of respect for teachers, not listening to teachers and guardians, not doing homework, running out of schools after break, watching TV at night, and going out for social events, including funerals. As any corporal punishment, including the use of cane, has been banned in Ghana since 2016, how to discipline pupils without using the cane has become a serious concern for school communities and schools.

RT in "Professional Capacity"

"Professional Capacity" is defined as the extent to which schools have an adequate quality and number of professional teachers and whether teachers (including the headteacher) have a common understanding to achieve educational outcomes. As mentioned earlier, according to the headteacher, most teachers have opted out transfer owing to the community divide. Teachers associated pupils' indiscipline with such divides in geographical and school communities and lamented this as follows: "Children also carry the same mentality with parents . . . Indiscipline comes from home too . . . If parents talk negatively about teachers, pupils do not listen to teaches at school" (D20170926TC).

At school D, the headteacher insisted that they needed to adhere to the directive as a unit of the local educational administration. However, teachers believed that it was necessary for the disciplining of pupils should be continued. One teacher described this situation as follows:

> As a teacher, I made a pupil who misbehaved stand outside the classroom but the headteacher said that I should not do that . . . If teachers do not get necessary support, teachers hesitate to do what they thought should do.
> (D20180920TC)

Another teacher described his experience as follows: "The use of cane is not necessarily must. But when my child did offense, I will warn them once and twice but next time I will tell them why you are caned and did it" (D20180920TC).

Views on how to discipline pupils differed between the headteacher and teachers at School D. Teachers placed more importance on showing their authority to discipline pupils – even using the cane, if necessary – because pupils' indiscipline was the most challenging issue for them.

Both headteachers in Schools A and D had the same view – that the teachers should not use the cane anymore and should find other ways of disciplining pupils. However, there were differences between Schools A and D in terms of how teachers reacted to their headteachers' views. While teachers at School A thought that pupils' discipline was secured, owing to collaboration between the geographical and school communities, teachers at School D had to rely on the cane as the last resort to discipline pupils.

RT in "Parent, School, Community Ties"

"Parent, School, Community Ties" includes both collective participation as members of school communities and individual participation as individual parents. School communities in both Schools A and D argued with the headteacher and teachers regarding how they responded to the government directive that banned any corporal punishment, including the use of the cane. However, there were clear differences between these two in terms of how they came to a consensus through dialogues and how they put their decisions into practice.

School A discussed at PTA general meetings the issue of pupils' disrespect for guardians at home and pupils' indiscipline. Guardians expected teachers to discipline pupils using the cane when they misbehaved. Some guardians argued that if the school adhered to the directive, they would be forced to transfer their children to other schools (CTA Meeting Minutes, A20180518).

Some teachers also objected to the directive and some referred to the Bible, which permits necessary punishment for misbehaving children. Other teachers doubted the effects of punishment without pain (e.g. raising their hands for five minutes), and they insisted that they could not agree with the banning of the cane (CTA Meeting Minutes, A20180518).

To respond to these arguments by guardians and teachers, the headteacher emphasized that they did not need to use the cane but rather advised that pupils, teachers, and guardians should have cordial relationships. They also explained that any corporal punishment would be illegal and that if teachers punished pupils, then guardians might sue teachers. Thus, they needed to find ways to discipline pupils without using the cane (CTA Meeting Minutes, A20180518).

After diverse and sometimes conflicting opinions expressed by the guardians, teachers, the headteacher, and a circuit supervisor, it appeared that guardians had the view that if pupils committed any offenses, guardians should be invited to school to understand why their children should be disciplined. This implies that school-level stakeholders at School A came to understand, after a series of discussions, that they should have dialogues without caning pupils.

In addition, the geographical communities for School A had functioned to reinforce the school communities' decisions over pupils' discipline to all the community members regardless of the existence of pupils. One SMC executive member mentioned this as follows:

During the PTA meeting, guardians requested teachers to give more homework to make pupils engaged with learning. In addition to that, they passed a resolution that no child is allowed to go to neighborhood to watch TV. If they do not adhere to this rule, those guardians will be sanctioned. Such decisions taken at the PTA meeting were conveyed to all the members in geographical communities through a community announcer using a megaphone (A20180919PA).

On the other hand, the school communities at School D did not have the opportunity to discuss pupils' discipline with the headteacher and teachers, and they could not agree on any measures to be taken owing to the community divide. The headteacher insisted that guardians should monitor their children to make sure that they did not go out at night and/or weekends or watch TV. Despite such appeals by the headteacher, pupils' indiscipline became more serious, without support from guardians and geographical communities. From the viewpoint of the teachers, pupils were affected by the community divide that their parents were engaged with.

Parents noticed that the PTA chairperson and the SMC chairperson came from the chief's side, and so parents on the other side did not come to meetings due to that reason. This affected children's learning greatly. Sometimes, due to this issue, some pupils did not appreciate themselves.

RT in "School Learning Climate" and "Pedagogy Factors"

"School Learning Climate" is regarded as the extent to which schools and classrooms are safe and orderly, in terms of the school atmosphere. "Pedagogical Factors" is considered to represent the extent of "Time for

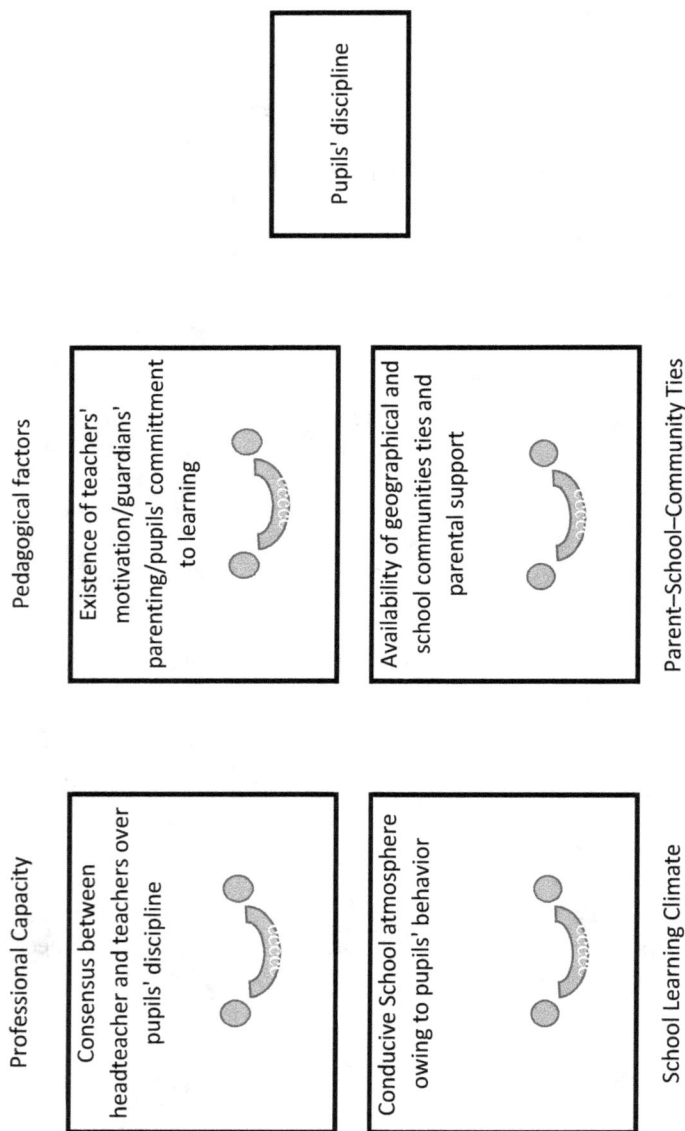

Professional Capacity

Pedagogical factors

Consensus between headteacher and teachers over pupils' discipline

Existence of teachers' motivation/guardians' parenting/pupils' committment to learning

Conducive School atmosphere owing to pupils' behavior

Availability of geographical and school communities ties and parental support

School Learning Climate

Parent–School–Community Ties

Pupils' discipline

Figure 5.29 Structure of how relationships between actors and factors in school management lead to pupils' discipline (School A). Developed by the author.

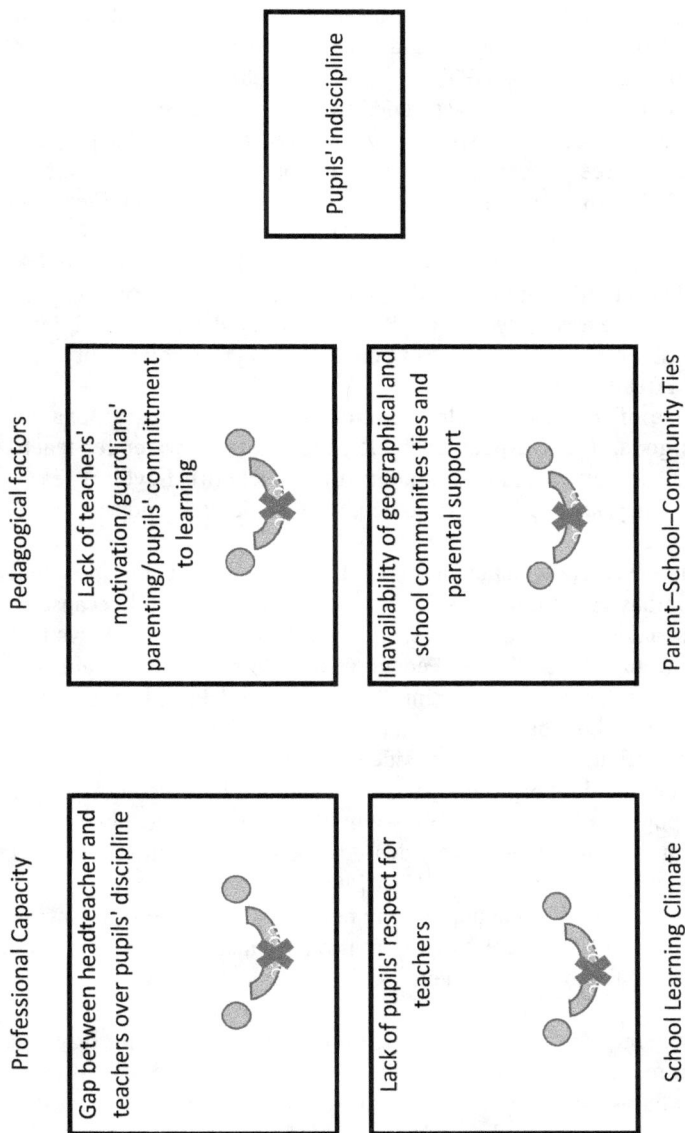

Figure 5.30 Structure of how relationships between actors and factors in school management lead to pupils' indiscipline (School D). Developed by the author.

Learning," "Supplementary Resources," and "Dynamics of Student Learning," composed of "Motivation" and "School Participation." As teachers and pupils are part of the instructional triangle, I considered motivation to include both "Teacher Motivation" and "Pupil Motivation."

In terms of "Teacher-parent RT," at School A, both teachers and parents regarded that pupils' discipline was good, owing to contributions from each side. One guardian recalled teachers' contributions to pupils' discipline as follows: "Pupils greet parents when they come back home, go, eat, and do homework. This is because teachers made impacts on pupils and teachers are more committed to do their work" (A20180919PA).

One pupil also stated that pupils were committed to learning at School A, as follows: "Discipline at this school is good. Pupils are attentive to teachers . . . . Before the assembly starts at 8am, we sweep the compound, fetch water for washing tanks, read English books. Pupils greet community people here" (A20180924PU).

Finally, one of the teachers also mentioned the followings: "Behavior of pupils is good. They respect teachers. Students fetch water for teachers (who stay in surrounding community of the school). Level of learning is good. They are ready to go to school on time and ready to learn" (A20170925TC).

These narratives show that guardians, pupils, and teachers at School A had unanimous views that the school's atmosphere was good because of the pupils' behavior and that they were ready for learning. This shows that "School Learning Climate" and "Pedagogical factors" were well aligned. This also implies that "Teacher-parent RT" over pupils' discipline was realized, as they expected others to play their responsibilities and felt obliged to make their contributions to the other side (Figure 5.29).

On the other hand, at School D, pupils' discipline has become a major issue. One pupil confessed the following: "Some pupils do not respect teachers because some overaged students work after the school (such as motor riders) and get some money" (D20180920PU).

Teachers also observed that pupils were not committed to learning owing to the lack of guardians' care and supervision from their guardians. One teacher made the following comment:

> If children are serious about picking up learning, it motivates teachers to do more. . . . Pupils do not see the necessity to learn. Some of them have textbooks but they are not serious about education, they watch TV at home without study . . . Parents should take care of their wards by providing their needs before they come to school. This will make children feel happy and concentrate on learning.
>
> (D20170926TC)

Teachers saw that the lack of guardians' support was behind the pupils' indiscipline. A teacher at School D mentioned as follows: "Indiscipline comes from home too. If parents talk negatively about teachers, pupils do not listen to teaches at school" (D20170926TC).

The guardians, headteacher, teachers, and pupils at School D all had the unanimous view that pupils, especially some overaged pupils, did not listen to and respect teachers. Teachers mentioned that pupils carried the same mentality with their guardians, who were divided owing to the community divide. Thus, "School Learning Climate" was affected by lack of "Parent, School, Community Ties."

The suspension of school excursions implied lack of a conducive "School Learning Climate." School excursions were discussed on the agenda, but were postponed owing to a lack of funds (June and October 2015; February and June 2016). The inability of School D to conduct school excursions demotivated pupils and teachers. A JHS grade three pupil recalled the suspension of school excursions as sad news and wished that it could take place again. One primary teacher shared that when she talked to her pupils about school excursions, they said that they did not have the money for the excursions. This implies that the suspension of school excursions, induced by lack of collective participation, seriously affected "Pedagogical factors" in terms of pupils' and teachers' motivation.

The community divide made the school communities lose their collective space to discuss the issues of pupils' discipline and its preventive measures at School D. This could have influenced individual parenting to discipline pupils as well. Without reinforcement from the geographical and school communities, as well as guardians' support, the teachers also felt vulnerable in coping with pupils' indiscipline (Figure 5.30).

References

Bryk, A. S., Sebring, P. B., Allensworth, E., Luppescu, S., & Easton, J.Q. (2010). *Organizing Schools for Improvement: Lessons from Chicago.* Chicago, IL: University of Chicago Press.
Ghana Education Service. (2012). *School management committee resource handbook.* Ghana Education Service.

6 Conclusions and discussions

Summary of findings

Based on the conceptual framework (Figure 6.1), I present the key findings that answer the following research questions:

Research Question 1) To what extent does community participation function in school management?

Research Question 2) To what extent are community participation, SES, educational outcomes, and RT related?

Research Question 3) How is RT realized between actors and in factors of school management to generate educational outcomes?

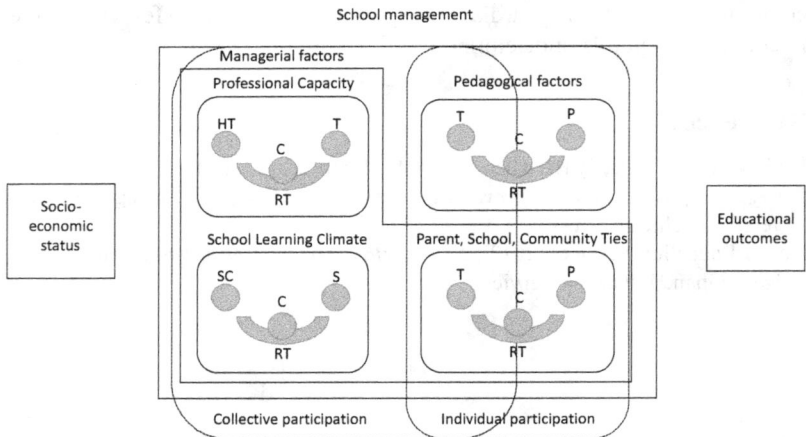

Figure 6.1 Conceptual framework. Developed by the author.

DOI: 10.4324/9781003320579-6

Regarding RQ1, this study shows that the approach of community participation with the principle of representative democracy was flawed, owing to the limited scope of the SPIP consultation and delays in the CG disbursement. Instead, community participation with the principle of consensual democracy was found to be active, in the form of the number of PTA general meeting participants and the amount of PTA funds. Essuman (2013) indicated that support from SMCs or PTAs filled the gap that was created as a result of government fiscal deficits and delays in the transfer of funds to schools. Findings from this study echoes with his statement. This implies that when we analyze community participation in school management, it is necessary to pay attention to not only the representative democracy for decision-making in school management, but also the consensual democracy, which has played a critical role in supporting schools since their establishment.

RQ2 and RQ3 are complementary in a sense that RQ2 examines the extent to which RT is related to educational outcomes and factors in school management through the quantitative analysis, while RQ3 addresses why such relationships occur through the qualitative analysis. First, I examined the relationship between RT and learning outcomes. The correlation analysis shows hat "Teacher-parent RT" is negatively related (statistically significant) to the BECE mean aggregate. This means that the higher the "Teacher-parent RT," the better the learning outcomes. Carolan-Silva (2011) pointed out that parents in rural areas in developing countries tended to prefer collective participation to individual participation, which required them to take care of pupils' learning at home. However, this study shows that "Teacher-parent RT," which dealt with individual participation, is related to better learning outcomes. The question why such a relationship occurred is addressed in the next paragraph.

The qualitative analysis gave some clues in which factors of school management RT should be realized to yield learning outcomes. The first qualitative case study sheds light on why a high-performing school in a rural area, experienced a rapid decline in its learning outcomes. It was found that the school was suffered from a community divide, owing to a dispute over the legitimacy of chieftaincy claim. The lack of "School communities-school RT' affected the extent of collective participation, which is one of the critical indicators of the "Parent, School, Community Ties' factor. This failure in managerial factors led to lack of support for school development, which affected the pedagogical factors – including "Time for learning," "Supplementary resources' and "Pupils' school participation." This appeared to result in decline in learning outcomes. In addition, the third case study showed that the lack of "Teacher-parent RT" was associated with the low extent of pupils' motivation, guardians' support and teachers' motivation. These were included in the "Pedagogical factors," which directly affects pupils' learning outcomes. These findings contributes to revealing why "Teacher-parent RT' is related to better learning outcomes.

Second, this study reveals that school enrollment depended on the extent of collective participation. In this study, to avoid correlations among independent variables, collective participation indicators were integrated into a composite collective participation indicator. The quantitative analysis showed that school enrollment is positively correlated (statistically significant) with the collective participation composite indicator. This showed that the larger the extent of collective participation, the larger the school enrollment. This appeared to be a common sense in urban areas, however, it is important for schools in rural areas to sustain or increase school enrollment. Increasing the school enrollment is also an important strategy for generating more collective participation in the form of PTA funds, which becomes a driver for school development.

The second qualitative case study showed how schools have sustained or increased school enrollment, while the other school, though in similar rural settings, experienced stagnated school enrollment. The headteacher developed an initiative to address the school's low enrollment. The school communities responded to the headteacher's expectations and mobilized resources for school development, in line with their obligations. Thus, "School communities-school RT' was realized in the "Parent, School, Community Ties' factor, which was equivalent to collective participation, namely, attending meetings and paying for PTA funds. With such collective participation after realization of the "School communities-school RT," it was possible for the school and the school communities to work toward improving school enrollment.

It was also found that the existence of "Headteacher-teacher RT' matters in promoting teachers' engagement with increased school enrollment. At School A, the headteacher expected teachers to improve their working attitude, conduct pedagogical activities for pupils to come to school without delay or absence. With the headteacher's leadership and commitment, teachers, in return, felt obliged to respond to such expectations by showing their commitment to pedagogical activities. Literature have argued that individual households' SES will affect the extent of their involvement in school affairs. However, this study reveals that school communities with less endowed SES could achieve some extent of collective participation through realizing RT. This can be interpreted as a survival strategy for socially and economically fragile individual households in developing countries to enjoy collective benefits through the participation in school communities.

Third, this study reveals how pupils' discipline was affected by each of the school management factors, depending on the realization of RT. The third qualitative case study showed how division in geographical communities caused declining "Parent, School, Community Ties," which resulted in lack of the "Pedagogical factors," such as the decreased motivations for teachers, guardians and pupils. The directive that banned corporal punishment, including the use of cane, affected all the schools in Ghana. However, the two case study schools enacted different responses in terms of pupils' discipline. It was found that these two schools had different levels of RT regarding whether they could avoid conflicts through dialogue with school-level stakeholders.

At School A, school-level stakeholders were able to reach a certain level of common understanding with regards to not using cane, as the results of thorough discussions at the school communities. The geographical communities also ensured that decision-making at the school communities was executed in all the households. In this school, where the managerial factors were functional, guardians, teachers and pupils unanimously put high value on pupils' discipline. On the other hand, School D, where the geographical communities were divided owing to a dispute over the legitimacy of chieftaincy claim, the managerial factors that the school communities had – meetings and mobilized resources – were in decline. Thus, the school communities could not have opportunities to discuss with the headteacher and teachers to find out solutions to pupils' discipline. This case study highlighted the significance of RT among school-level stakeholders on pupils' discipline.

Contribution to literature

This study aims to fill in research gaps and findings from this study contributes to the literature from both theoretical and practical perspectives: 1) how RT links factors and actors in school management to yield educational outcomes; 2) how RT occurs as the mutual accountability among school-level stakeholders; 3) how RT is perceived as an interplay among participation, leadership and accountability; 4) how RT can make pupils the subject of learning; and 5) how RT can bridge the relationship between the individual households and collectives of school communities. Narratives are described below from both the theoretical perspective and the practical perspective.

RT as a "harness" with actors and factors in school management toward educational outcomes

There is a research gap in the literature regarding the mechanism through which community participation in school management will lead to educational outcomes. Particularly, it is still unknown how managerial and pedagogical factors should be linked to yield educational outcomes, especially in the context of developing countries that are experiencing severe resource scarcity.

This study shows that what could determine these differences was whether a chain of RT between actors occurred in the factors of school management or not. In three case studies comparing two schools with differences in attainment of educational outcomes, if RT is realized in one factor as synchronies in mutual expectations and obligations among actors, it can induce RT in other factors in school management, then leads to educational outcomes. This is how RT is formulated as a harness with actors and factors in the process of school management.

RT as "mutual accountability" among guardians, school communities, school, and government

Studies have criticized the accountability framework presented by the World Development Report 2003 as a one-way accountability route from parents to schools (Nishimura, 2018). However, there is a research gap in the literature regarding how the mutual accountability occurs among various school-level stakeholders, and in which relationships it occurs.

This study suggests that it is necessary for school communities not only to expect schools to perform their duties but also to feel obliged to support schools and teachers. The case of School B showed that school communities agreed to implement the actions discussed at the PTA meetings, but could not put them into practice. The case of School D also showed that school excursions were suspended owing to lack of collective participation, despite frequent discussions over the topic. This finding is in line with Nishimura (2018) who empahsized the significance of the mutual accountability, where school-level stakeholders should be both clients and service providers. Thus, this finding suggests that in order to realize RT, school communities should be accountable to schools for providing support, in tandem with having expectations for the schools.

School A's case showed that, with synchronies in expectations and obligations from the school communities to the school, the headteacher developed his initiative to improve school enrollment in collaboration with teachers. As a result, the school communities members became aware of the school's improved enrollment, which they attributed to the school's contribution. The difference between Figure 4.2 and Figure 6.2 is that obligations from one side to the other side will not occur automatically because expectations from the other side are given, but rather because both expectations and obligations from each side make obligations from the other side occur. This provides an important implication for school communities in developing countries under resource scarcity. When school communities have expected

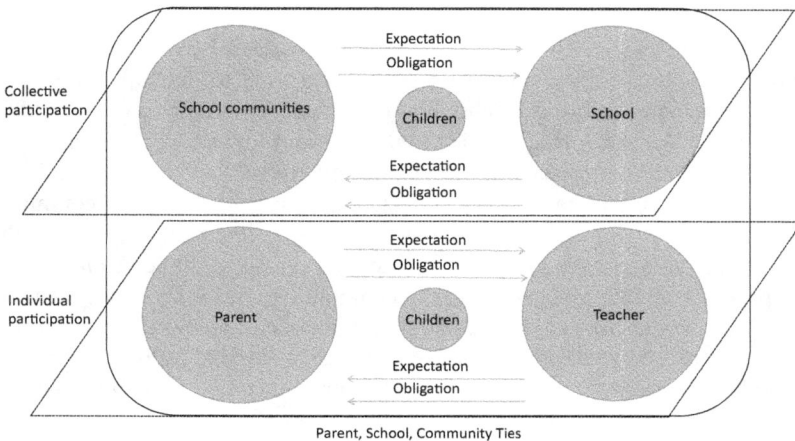

Figure 6.2 How RT is realized with children being at the center both at collective and individual participation. Developed by the author.

schools for perform, their expectations must be accompanied by their obligations to headteacher and teachers. Under such circumstances, headteacher and teachers feel obliged to be accountable to the school communities for performing their expected duties. In summary, this study contributes to filling in research gaps regarding how mutual accountability among school-level stakeholders will occur through the realization of RT.

RT as an "interplay" among leadership, participation, and accountability

There exists a research gap regarding how leadership, participation and accountability will work in tandem in role relationships and factors in school management.

This study reveals that leadership, participation and accountability should be interpreted as a series of perceived expectations and/or obligations in each RT. For instance, the first case study showed that without community leadership and support, teachers did not feel obliged to play their expected roles to enhance pupils' learning, and to be accountable to the school communities for pupils' performance. In the second case study, the headteacher initiated his leadership on sustaining school enrollment, and expected the school communities to mobilize PTA funds for school development. The school communities in return mobilized PTA funds via collective participation and showed their accountability to the headteacher's leadership.

The third case study revealed a sharp comparison between schools in terms of the availability of RT, shown as the nexus of leadership, participation and accountability. At School A, the headteacher took his leadership to consider measures to discipline pupils without the use of cane, and the school communities discussed issues collectively and became accountable to such leadership by reinforcing collective decisions of the school communities to all the geographical community members. On the contrary, School D was not able to have a collective space to discuss pupils' discipline and its preventive measures, owing to the community divide. Thus, despite the headteacher's leadership, participation did not occur, nor was accountability put in place to respond to such leadership. In summary, this study contributes to revealing how leadership, participation and accountability work in tandem in role relationships, and in the factors of school management. It also contributes to answering a question raised by Taniguchi and Hirakawa (2016) as to what develops teachers' responsibilities to produce higher student achievements, and how school leadership and community leadership influence community participation in school management.

RT as a "catalyst" to make students the subject of learning

There is a research gap regarding how students will be motivated to learn as the subject of learning through the interaction with the school communities, the headteacher, the teachers and their guardians.

This study reveals that students are motivated to come to school and learn when RT is realized with students being at the centre of synchronies in mutual expectations and obligations, both at the levels of collective and individual participation as shown in Figure 6.2. The contrast between Schools A and D was that pupils' motivation will be affected by the availability of the "School communities-school RT," as well as "Teacher-parent RT." There are consistent perception gaps between teachers and parents in terms of participation in the pedagogical aspect. Carolan-Silva (2011) found that teachers were critical of parents' lack of participation in children's education at home, while parents felt that it was difficult to teach pupils at home because they did not understand what the pupils were learning. Thus, it is crucial to determine how to bridge such a gap between parents and teachers.

This study reveals that if RT works in managerial and pedagogical factors with children being at the centre, it encourages teachers and guardians to have reciprocal relationships for the benefit of pupils, which also motivates pupils to be engaged with schooling. As described in the case studies in the Chapter 5, pupils' motivation to learn or come to school is vital in enhancing learning outcomes or increasing enrollment. Studies have argued that parents/guardians and community members can hold headteacher/teachers accountable for their performance. However, pupils were not included in the scope of literature, and had only been discussed as the object of learning, represented as aggregated learning achievement or school enrollment. Thus, this study contributes to unpacking the significance of RT, which can make pupils as the subject of learning.

RT as a "mechanism" that makes individual households under diversity and fragility formulate a community of interdependence

A further critical research gap concerns knowing whether social capital exists within school communities or wider geographical community and knowing how the individual households and school communities interact with each other for the benefit of pupils. This study reveals the complexity of politics within geographical communities and the potentials of education toward community empowerment.

Complexity of politics within geographical communities

This study reveals that school communities would not work without the solid foundation of geographical communities. For instance, Schools B and D in case studies showed that geographical communities do not necessarily maintain a sense of collectivity, which seriously affected school communities. It appeared as a divide among guardians, among pupils, and between teachers and pupils. This finding resonates with what Pryor (2005) argued in the case of Ghana. According to him, social capital is not necessarily inherent within the community collectively owing to migration and the disintegration of matrilineal family structure, rather, social capital is used to further the interests of individual families.

At School D, where geographical communities do not meet and mobilize resources for their annual festival owing to the chieftaincy issue, there is the limitation of schooling that is buttressed with a sense of togetherness toward shared goals for educating children. Politics within geographical communities are historically rooted and stem from the conflicts over ethnicity, the political power balance, and the history, ownership, and location of schools. Though international literature has not touched on this aspect, this study acknowledges the complexity of politics within geographical and school communities as important contextual background.

Moreover, this study suggests the potential of RT in schooling toward community cohesion. Heyneman (2003) outlines the contributions of schools to social cohesion in the following perspectives: teaching rule of games, decreasing the distance between individuals of different origins, providing equal opportunities for all students and incorporating the interests and objectives of different groups and providing a common underpinning for citizenship. Komatsu (2014) posited the schools' role of promoting social cohesion in Bosnia and Herzegovina where different ethnic groups had civil wars in the past and are still undergoing the process of reconciliation. Edwards (2019) warned against the instrumental approach of community participation for the sake of educational outcomes. He emphasized that it is necessary to shift from the community involvement in schooling to the educational development as an element of community empowerment. The third case study showed that the instrumental approach would not work and community cohesion must be built first to realize RT in schooling. Findings from this study resonate with the literature in a sense that educational outcomes in a divisive community should include an aspect of social cohesion among different groups, which contributes to community empowerment or community reconstruction. It will also be a positive sign at School D that the youth, graduates from the school, came together to meet and talk with both sides of the chiefs and elders to resolve the chieftaincy issue. Thus, this study contributes to revealing that education has the potential of being the process of mutual understanding among the other, and that the existence of pupils and the youth as products of education plays key roles for community cohesion.

Social capital and RT

This study reveals that it matters how to manage conflicts through executing interdependence at each relationship within school communities more than just belonging to school communities as social capital theory asserts. Both School A and D faced conflicts over pupil discipline, which may result in unexpected consequences of pupil transfer or teacher transfer. This is critical because decreasing school enrollment is a challenge for School A while losing qualified teachers would worsen declined learning outcomes at School D. However, they made differences in managing such conflicts at each relationship; between geographical communities and school management: between teachers and guardians/pupils; and between headteacher and teachers.

This is an important finding to social capital theory which various developed and developing countries have relied on in the establishment of democratic institutions such as SMCs. As Selle and Kristin (1999) and Suetomi (2005) argued, social capital has been built on Putanam's notion of participatory democracy and has faced the following challenges. First, while Putnam assumed that people were willing to join collectives of community autonomously, parents, especially in urban areas do not feel the necessity of collective actions because they are occupied with their work or because they can support their child individually. Second, equal membership requires the same burden on their members, regardless of their work and circumstances. This becomes challenging for households working in double harness, who do not have time to engage themselves with school matters. Third, under such circumstances, while core members in parent associations may be actively engaged with school management, others may be busy with their jobs, and may therefore become marginalized because they are not actively involved in school activities. Nyamnjoh (2016) asserted that in African societies incomplete individuals formulate collectives of community with diverse backgrounds in a flexible manner in which individuals depend on each other. These characteristics of social capital differ from those of Putnam. Although more studies are necessary for generalization in African societies, this study contributes to revealing that social capital in African rural context needs to consider their fragility, diversity and flexibility, thereby illuminating RT as an analytical lens of the extent and the quality of inderdependence among school-level stakeholders.

This study also shows that individual households' awareness and actions are generated through discussions and consensus at collective spaces. This means that while fragile individual households participate in school communities to look for social capital as a collective goods, social capital generated at collective spaces will affect individual households' awareness and actions for improving their child at home and their preparation for pupils' school participation. It is worthwhile to investigate further how guardians' awareness of collective and individual participation are related. In summary, this study contributes to revealing how RT can bridge the relationship between the individual households under diversity and fragility, and the collectives of school communities, thereby overcoming challenges of social capital theory.

Implication for the system of community participation in school management

This study reveals that there are flaws in the institutionalized community participation in school management in Ghana, based on the participatory democracy of Western society, while the indigenous geographical communities were still playing an active role in supporting schools. This study provides some operational implications for community participation in school management in Ghana and other countries as follows.

Need to formulate RT by matching capable headteachers with supportive school communities

This study shows that headteacher' leadership is significant in realizing RT with school communities and teachers in both managerial and peda- gogical factors. The teaching profession in the basic education sector in Ghana is often considered to be a stepping-stone for future careers. A head- teacher's position does not appear to be attractive for teachers, due to the lack of incentives and the difficulties that they face. Experienced teachers tend to work in urban schools, considering their life environment. Okitsu and Edwards (2017) argued that volunteer teachers in Zambia do not have a sense of accountability to parents or the community, owing to teachers' survival needs: severe livelihood and lack of reliable transportation for commuting. Thus, it is critical to match capable headteachers with school communities that can support headteachers so as to overcome their survival needs. Such support may attract headteachers to be deployed to rural areas. For instance, providing free accommodation closer to schools appears to be effective for headteachers, because it can reduce accommodation and transportation costs. The district education offices can deploy even younger, but capable headteachers to rural schools, with the condition that geographi- cal and school communities promise to support headteacher's accommoda- tion. Capacity building opportunities will also be helpful for headteachers to develop relationships with their teachers, as well as geographical and school communities.

Need to retain RT as multiple sets of mutual accountability

This study reveals that realizing RT is identical to fulfilling mutual account- ability in various relationships among school-level stakeholders. Thus, it is necessary to have the multiple sets of mutual accountability for bet- ter school management and improved educational outcomes. Taking the accountability framework of the WDR 2003 into consideration of education sector, it is assumed that while schools receive the government CG, schools are expected to be accountable to school communities using the CG effec- tively to achieve educational outcomes. However, this study shows that this assumption did not hold true, owing to the delayed disbursement and the limited amount of the CG. In addition, if geographical and school communi- ties do not support schools through mobilizing various resources, schools do not feel obliged to perform their expected duties, thus failing to realize RT. Therefore, to hold schools accountable to both the government and school communities, it is necessary for the government and school communities not only to expect schools to perform better, but also to support schools.

This study shows that schools can hold school communities accountable for promoting school construction or introducing school feeding programs. In this case, mutual accountability, in which both schools and school communities are held accountable to each other, is key as the literature emphasize. There are multiple possibilities for the mutual accountability, depending on the following source of revenues: DA's Common Funds, PTA funds, town development committee funds and support from related stakeholders. In summary, multiple sets of mutual accountability are critical for schools and school communities to sustain daily school management, without solely depending on the CG.

Need to sustain a chain of RT in the existing system of institutionalized community participation

Following the theoretical claim in this Chapter, it is also necessary to sustain a chain of conducts, composed of leadership, participation, and accountability in the operation. In other words, it is necessary to sustain a chain of RT, which is composed of synchronies in mutual expectations and obligations in the existing system of institutionalized community participation. As mentioned in the Chapter 5, the institutionalized mechanism of community participation has venues to meet, discuss, and make decisions in school management like the SMC or PTA general meetings and the SPAM. When a headteacher or SMC or PTA chairperson showed the leadership to improve school learning climate, or professional capacity or pedagogical aspects at a SMC or PTA general meeting, it is necessary for school communities to agree on shared goals of school development/improvement.

Then, such expectations or agreements must be accompanied with obligations or conducts to make expectations come true by teachers' commitment to headteacher's leadership, or school communities' participation (collecting PTA funds through parents' contributions, providing labour works, sharing information to obtain support from local education offices or local governments). When school communities provide their obligations for schools, they also have expectations for schools to perform better or to address what schools can do. School communities want to know at another PTA or SMC general meeting how their contributions have worked toward the shared goals and why their shared goals are achieved or not. The SPAM, where the BECE results are mainly shared and discussed, is a possible venue to make school-level stakeholders accountable to each other for how expectations were met with obligations and vice-verse for the sake of improving pupils' learning. Utilizing the existing system of institutionalized community participation, a chain of RT should be sustained through keeping the synchronies in mutual expectations and obligations.

Need to support pupils as the subject of learning through
realizing RT at both collective and individual level

As suggested in this Chapter, it is necessary to support pupils as the subject of learning, at both collective and individual participation. In collective participation, pupils' participation in the SPAM appears to be effective. As shown in the case studies, the possible topics that pupils discuss at the SPAM may include "School learning climate (need to renovate classrooms)", "Professional capacity (need to fill in vacant teachers)', "Community, School, Parent Ties' (need to revive school excursions with support from parents and community) and "Pedagogical factors' (need to have extra classes for BECE). According to the monthly reports issued by the JICA-supported project in Burkina Faso, pupils and parents shared their commitments to achieving better learning outcomes at meetings like SPAM. This implies that pupils, as the subject of learning, need to be committed to learning, with support from teachers and guardians. It is possible for pupils to be motivated for learning when they are situated in improved learning environment, which can be provided through the collective participation by the school communities.

Carolan-Silva (2011) argues that parents deliberately prefer collective participation to individual participation owing to their weak academic background. It is difficult to grasp precisely the extent to which individual participation was implemented. Therefore, the way in addressing individual participation should be carefully considered. First, the way of individual participation among guardians, teachers, and pupils should be reconsidered in a way that parents feel comfortable without fears and concerns. For example, it appears to be difficult for guardians without educational backgrounds to understand aggregated figures such as enrollment rate/drop-out rate/completion rates, pass rates or correct answer rates at the school level. "Teaching at the Right Level," a method used by an Indian NGO, Pratham, appears to be useful for making such data easy to understand for guardians. Pratham aims to make children acquire foundational skills (arithmetic/reading) and shows the results to guardians by way of a simple literacy assessment tool. It classifies pupils to the following five levels: Beginner, Letter, Word, Paragraph and Story (Pratham, n.d.). This enables guardians to understand at which level their children are located, in terms of their learning progress.

This study suggests that homework appears to be an effective tool at individual participation, thereby engaging pupils with learning and facilitating communication among teachers, pupils, and guardians. According to the project monthly reports, the JICA-supported project in Burkina Faso made its trials in which parents checked the completion of their children's homework, without checking its pedagogical contents. This appeared to help children with doing homework as learning habits, helped parents without academic backgrounds to supervise homework, and helped to provide opportunities for parents and children to talk about school life and academic performance.

Need to support fragile individuals and school communities to sustain RT

This study informs local educational administrations of what they should monitor and support to mitigate educational disparities. In Ghana and many other countries, the EMIS questionnaire is administered every year. In Ghana, there are only the following four questions in terms of community participation in school management: whether there are SMCs elected by elections; how frequently SMC meetings are organized; whether the SPIP is formulated; and whether schools received the CG in the previous year. What this study reveals is that "Amount of mobilized PTA funds" and "Amount of mobilized PTA funds per enrollment' have positive and statistically significant correlations with the BECE mean aggregate. Therefore, if district education offices can monitor such indicators, they may be able to identify vulnerable schools that need more support.

It is also critical for local governments or local educational administration staff to identify whether geographical communities have troubles, such as community divides. Circuit supervisors, who are assigned to each circuit, appear to be effective in collecting such data, because they attend SMC/PTA executive and/or general meetings. This information should be gathered to identify necessary measures that could be taken to avoid worsening community divides. In a politically divisive situation like School D, political interventions may be necessary as ways of finding solutions to the challenges. As the District Director of Education, Akatsi South mentioned, the District Education Oversight Committee (DEOC), to which the District Chief Executive belong, may function to address the community divide because this is something beyond educational issues.

It is also significant to pay attention to fragile households within school communities. As explained in this study, most guardians in rural Ghana are socially and economically fragile, and are not homogeneous in terms of the biological relationship with children. Their commitment to and involvement with schooling appeared to be diverse owing to their circumstance. Thus, it is critical for these fragile households to participate in collective spaces, such as SMC or PTA general meetings, because they can depend on collective agencies to supplement their weak engagement at individual participation. As shown in these case studies, divisions in geographical communities severely affects school communities as spaces for collective participation. This gives a great impact on fragile households, who do not have a strong sense of individual participation at home and need to resort to collective participation via school communities.

Limitations

In this study, I collected data on RT in each role relationship from the perspective of headteachers. This was because I wanted to collect both the community participation data at schools and the RT data from headteachers, to the extent possible. However, there are several limitations in this study.

First, the headteacher questionnaire had the ceiling effects in various question items. I assume that this was because only headteachers answered the questionnaire to represent each school, meaning that there was little variance in their answers. If there are teachers' or guardians' questionnaires, it would be likely to have variance because they would have more respondents.

Second, "School communities-school RT" question items need to be reconsidered because there might be ambiguity as to what school communities means. I aimed to include parents and community members within school communities, however, respondents may interpret them as comprising the SMC/PTA executive members who always meet and discuss with headteachers. In such a case, perceptions of the SMC/PTA executive members may differ from those of the parents and community members. School B had a relatively high extent of "School communities-school RT" but had low collective participation. This might have arisen owing to such perception gaps.

Third, relationships among school-level stakeholders are more complex, and need to be examined more carefully. For instance, in Figure 6.2, I could not analyze the relationship between the school communities as a collective and parents as individuals. In addition, it is still unknown as to how teachers as a collective will affect individual teacher's consciousness, attitude, and behavior.

Fourth, the data on factors in school management were limited. As Bryk et al. (2010) conducted, such data should have been collected thoroughly in order to investigate the relationships between factors in school management and RT. In addition, more of the qualitative data should have been collected in the longer time frame. I analyzed the realization of RT as synchronies in mutual expectations and obligations within certain years, based on available data. However, it may be too early to determine whether RT is realized or not over time and became stronger or weaker. Observations should be made regarding how RT builds on factors and among school-level stakeholders as accumulated assets over time.

Fifth, this study did not conduct in-depth analysis of cultural communities. As case study schools are located in rural areas in the Akatsi South District, the population was dominated by one ethnic group, Ewe, thus, I did not pay much attention to that aspect. However, if it comes to urban areas in Ghana, people from different ethnic groups are mixed up and coexist. Thus, consideration into ethnic identity needs to be reflected in the future research design if the study must deal with diverse cultural communities.

Suggestions for further study

Several suggestions can be raised for further study. First, there is a need to conduct a continuous qualitative study to trace whether RT is realized over time. Careful examination is also needed regarding how RT is realized, and how RT will be accumulated to induce collective participation and educational outcomes. Thus, continuous qualitative study is necessary to trace the process among RT, collective participation, and educational outcomes.

Second, the relationships among community development, RT, and educational outcomes should be explored further. It may affect community' engagement with education how community has been traditionally consensual in terms of community development and the value of education. Declining educational outcomes may be one of the symbolic phenomena to be addressed, however, without solving root causes for community divide, the instrumental approach of community participation will not work.

Third, more data should be collected as to how pupils' consciousness, attitude and behaviors are affected as the result of community participation at the collective level, as well as parents' participation and their interactions with teachers at the individual level. This is an area where little research has been conducted, and it needs to be further explored.

Fourth, further examination is needed as to whether the conceptual framework of this study will be relevant in different contexts within Ghana (different regions, private schools, and public schools in urban areas) as well as in other countries.

Fifth, consideration into politics within geographical and school communities needs to have more attention in the study of community participation in school management. Any interventions in schooling and community development in general, are defined and viewed from the political perspectives of stakeholders, who are concerned about ethnicity, political power balance, and decision-making over resource mobilization and/ or allocation.

Concluding note

This study aims to analyze the relationships between actors and factors in school management from the viewpoint of RT. Community participation in school management, institutionalized in Western society, has relied on Putnam (2000)'s social capital theory at the collective level that independent households participate in civil society autonomously, share equal responsibilities, and formulate collectives of community. However, in view of diversity and fragility of individual households in African society, the assumption of social capital theory does not necessarily exist. This study contributes to illuminating RT as an analytical lens how individual households under resource scarcity and with diverse background formulate collectives of interdependence. Through participation in collectives of school communities, it was possible that RT, which comprise the synchronies in mutual expectations and obligations, is realized and individual households supplement their scarce resources together as the result of collective actions. Finally, this study presents important implications for community participation in school management mechanism not only in developed countries but also in industrialized countries because their societies become diversified in parents' working modality, and disparities are widened among households in terms of involvement with school affairs.

References

Carolan-Silva, A. (2011). Negotiating the roles of community members and parents: Participation in education in rural Paraguay. *Comparative Education Review*, *55*(2), 252–270.

Edwards Jr., D. B. (2019). Shifting the perspective on community-based management of education: From systems theory to social capital and community empowerment. *International Journal of Educational Development*, *64*, 17–26.

Essuman, A. (2013). *Decentralization of education management in Ghana: Key issues in school-community relations*. LAP LAMBERT Academic Publishing.

Heyneman, S. (2003). Social cohesion, and the future role of international organizations. *Peabody of Journal of Education*, *78*(3), 25–39.

Komatsu, T. (2014). Does decentralization enhance a school's role of promoting social cohesion? Bosnian school leaders' perceptions of school governance. *International Review of Education*, *60*, 7–31.

Nishimura, M. (2017). Community participation in school management in developing countries. *Oxford Research Encyclopedia of Education*. https://doi.org/10.1093/acrefore/9780190264093.013.64

Nishimura, M. (2018). Community participation in school governance: The Massai community in Kenya. *Prospects*. https://doi.org/10.1007/s11125-018-9439-8

Nyamnjoh, F. B. (2016). Incompleteness: Frontier Africa and the currency of conviviality (K. Kusunoki & M. Matsuda, Trans.). In M. Matsuda & M. Hirano-Nomoto (Eds.), *Cultural creativity for conflict resolution and coexistence:*

African potentials as practice of incompleteness and bricolage (pp. 311–347). Kyoto University Press.

Okitsu, T., & Edwards Jr, B. D. (2017). Policy promise and the reality of community involvement in school-based management in Zambia: Can the rural poor hold schools and teachers to account? *International Journal of Educational Development, 56*, 28–41.

Pratham. (n.d.). www.pratham.org/programs/education/elementary/

Pryor, J. (2005). Can community participation mobilize social capital for improvement of rural schooling? A case study from Ghana. *Compare, 35*(2), 193–203.

Putnam, R. D. (2000). *Bowing alone: The collapse and revival of American community.* Simon & Schuster.

Selle, P., & Kristin, S. (1999). Organizational membership and democracy: Do we need to consider passive members seriously? (Ogawa, A). University of Chiba. *Journal of Law and Politics, 14*(1), 143–166.

Suetomi, K. (2005). Public schools as club goods and their membership issues: Position of passive members in decentralized education reforms. *Japan Educational Administration Society Bulletin, 31*, 133–150.

Taniguchi, K., & Hirakawa, Y. (2016). Dynamics of community participation, student achievement and school management: The case of primary schools in a rural area of Malawi. *Compare, 46*(3), 479–502.

Appendices

Appendix 1. Framework of essential support for improvement

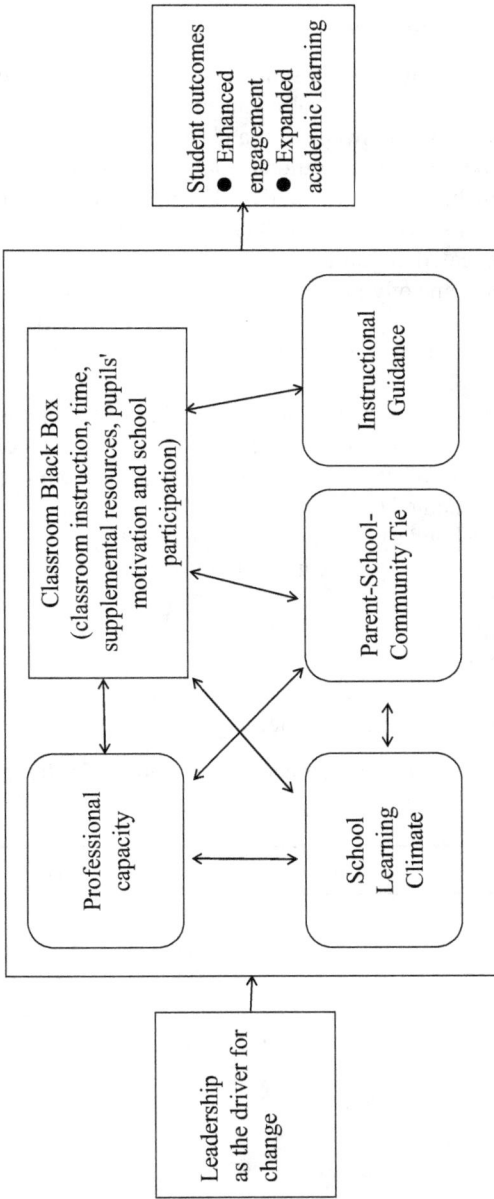

Appendix 2: Headteacher questionnaire

Headteachers' questionnaire

This questionnaire is to understand the status quo of headteachers, teachers at your schools, and the following relationships: between school communities and school; between you and teachers; among teachers; between teachers and parents. This should be completed by the school head or in his/her absence by his/her representative. The information gathered through the questionnaire is strictly used for this research only. Individual information will not be revealed in public.

Answer the name of your school:_____

1   About yourself and your school

SELF1 1–1. What is your sex?   □Male   □Female
SELF2 1–2. How old are you?   _____ years old
SELF3 1–3. What is the highest level of academic qualification you have attained?
□Junior secondary education or equivalent
□Senior secondary education or equivalent
□Certificate A
□Diploma
□Bachelor
□Master
□Non-teaching certificate/degree

1–4. Describe your teacher career history and fill in the table (Refer to an example)

From	Until	Name of school

Refer to the example below.
(Example)

From	Until	Name of school
2002		Graduated from St. Francis COE
2002	2005	Appointed as teacher and deployed to Zuta Basic schools
2005	2008	Transferred to Akatsi Demonstration primary school
2008	2010	Study leave at University of Cape Coast (Bachelor)
2010	Now	Transferred to Akatsi No. 1 JHS
2015	Now	Promoted to headteacher at Akatsi No. 1 JHS

SELF7 1–5. Have you had any orientation or training since you were appointed as a headteacher?
□Yes   □No

SELF8 If yes, when was the recent training that you participated?(_____)

1–6. Fill in enrollment data at your school over the past three years in the following table.

	FY2014/2015	FY2015/2016	FY2016/2017
KG: Male			
KG: Female			
Prim: Male			
Prim: Female			
JHS: Male			
JHS: Female			
Total			

2   Teachers at your school

2–1. How many teachers do you have at this school?

TKGM KG: Male____teachers **TKGF** Female____teachers **TKGT**
TPMM Prim: Male____teachers **TPMF** Female____teachers **TPMT**
TJHSM JHS: Male____teachers **TJHSF** Female____teachers **TJHST**
TTOTAL Total:_____

2–2. How many teachers at your school are paid by the followings?

TGES 1. GES:_____teachers
TDA 2. DA:_____teachers

TCP 3. Community and/or parents:_____teachers

TG 4. Government (Youth Employment Program and national service):_____teachers

TO 5. Others:_____teachers

2–3. How many teachers fall into the following in terms of years working as teaching professionals?

TY04 1.0–4 years:___teachers **TY59** 2.5–9 years:___teachers
TY1014 3.10–14 years:__teachers **TY1519** 4.15–19 years:__teachers
TY2024 5.20–24 years:__teachers **TY2529** 6.25–29 years:__teachers
TY3034 7.30–34 years:__teachers **TY35** 8. More than 35 years:__teachers

2–4. How many teachers fall into the following as years working for your school?

TE02 1.0–2 years:___teachers **TE35** 2.3–5 years:___teachers
TE68 3.6–8 years:___teachers **TE810** 4.8–10 years:___teachers
TE10 5. More than 10 years:___teachers

2–5. How many teachers of your school fall into the following age group?

TA 21 1. below 21:__teachers **TA 2125** 2.21–25 years:__teachers
TA 2630 3.26–30 years:__teachers **TA 3135** 4.31–35 years:_teachers
TA 3640 5.36–40 years:__teachers **TA 4145** 6.41–45 years:__teachers
TA 4650 7.46–50 years:__teachers **TA 5155** 8.51–55 years:__teachers
TA 5660 9.56–60 years:_teachers **TA MORE35** 10. More than 35 years: __teachers

2–6. How many teachers have attained the following as highest level of academic qualification?

TQ1 1. Junior secondary education or equivalent:__teachers
TQ2 2. Senior secondary education or equivalent:___teachers
TQ3 3. Certificate A:___teachers
TQ4 4. Diploma:___teachers
TQ5 5. Bachelor:___teachers
TQ6 6. Master:___teachers
TQ7 7. Non-teaching certificate/degree:___teachers

2–7. How many teachers fall into the following regarding their way of commuting to the school?

TC1 1. Commute from community surrounding the school:__teachers
TC2 2. Commute from nearby villages:__teachers
TC3 3. Commute from nearby towns:__teachers
TC4 4. Commute from long distance beyond nearby towns:__teachers

3   Collective participation by school communities (community members and parents)

Answer the following questions.

CP1 3–1. Does your school develop SPIP?
☐Every year without delay   ☐Every year but with delay
☐Not every year   ☐Not at all
CP131
CP2 3–2. How does your school discuss the content of SPIP before submitting it to the District Education office? (you may tick as many as possible)
☐Discuss within school staff
☐Discuss with SMC chairperson
☐Discuss with SMC or PTA executive members
☐Discuss with parents and community members at SMC or
PTA general meetings
CP3 3–3. When is the capitation grant normally disbursed to school account in the first term?
☐Just when SPIP activities start
☐nearly half of way in the implementation of SPIP activities
☐when SPIP activities is going to end
☐after SPIP activities end or later

3–4. Fill in the following table by describing information about the extent of community participation (frequency of SMC or PTA meeting, number of participants, amount of mobilized PTA funds) over three years referring to the past SMC or PTA minutes.

	FY2014/2015	*FY2015/2016*	*FY2016/2017*
CP4SMCE Frequency of SMC executive meetings			
CP4PTAE Frequency of PTA executive meetings			
CP4SMCG Frequency of SMC general meetings			

	FY2014/2015	FY2015/2016	FY2016/2017
CP4PTAG Frequency of PTA general meetings			
CP4SMCP Number of participants at each SMC general meetings			
CP4PTAP Number of participants at each PTA general meetings			
CP4PTALP Number of parents who paid PTA funds against that of parents who are supposed to pay (**CP4PTALSP**)			
CP4PTAL Amount of capitation grant delivered to school account in total per year			
CP4CG Amount of mobilized PTA funds per year			
CP4SPAM Frequency of SPAM per year			

Note: If SMC and PTA organize their meetings jointly, put in one column and indicate its frequency and number of participants as joint meetings

4   Relationship between school communities and school (headteacher and teachers)

Note: school communities are defined here as a group of local stakeholders who are parents/guardians and community members participating in and involving in SMC or PTA activities.

Tick most appropriate answers or describe your opinions in the following questions.

SC1 4–1. As a headteacher, how do you want this school and your students to be? In other words, what is your vision for the development of the school and students? Describe in the following space.

SC2 4–2. I communicate with /appeal to the school communities on the above-mentioned vision and necessary support at SMC or PTA general meetings

☐Always   ☐Often   ☐Sometimes   ☐Not at all

SC3 4–3. What kind of resource channels does your school have in terms of support for school development over the past three years? (you may tick as many as possible)

☐ 1 Capitation grant
☐ 2 Educational supplies by GES district office
☐ 3 DA support for school infrastructure
☐ 4 PTA funds
☐ 5 Communal labor by parents and/or community members
☐ 6 Support from chief/elders (such as provision of land)
☐ 7 Support from graduated students including those who are living in cities or abroad
☐ 8 NGO support
☐ 9 Donation from individuals, philanthropists, companies, public or private organizations/associations
☐10 Internally generated funds
☐11 Others (Specify:)

SC4 4–4. Which resource channels from the above are most reliable for your school? Indicate the number below. If you have multiple answers, indicate them in their priority order (that are more reliable comes far left and the second comes on its right)

SC5 4–5. School communities provide necessary support for students' development and learning at the school

☐Strongly agree   ☐Agree   ☐Disagree   ☐Strongly disagree

SC6 4–6. What kind of support (material and labor) were available to the school from school communities over the past three years? Describe in the following space.

SC7 4–7. School communities provide necessary support for teachers
☐Strongly agree ☐Agree ☐Disagree ☐Strongly disagree

SC8 4–8. What kind of support (financial, material, and labor) were available to teachers from school communities over the past three years? Describe in the following space.

{ }

4–9. School communities consult with the school when they have concerns about students and their education
☐Strongly agree ☐Agree ☐Disagree ☐Strongly disagree

4–10. School communities pay serious attention to whatever the school informs them of what happened to as well as what will be necessary for the school and students
☐Strongly agree ☐Agree ☐Disagree ☐Strongly disagree

4–11. School communities participate in SMC or PTA general meetings actively
☐Strongly agree ☐Agree ☐Disagree ☐Strongly disagree

4–12. School communities understand concerns by the school about students' development and their learning
☐Strongly agree ☐Agree ☐Disagree ☐Strongly disagree

4–13. Talking with school communities help the school (headteacher and teachers) to understand them better
☐Strongly agree ☐Agree ☐Disagree ☐Strongly disagree

4–14. Teachers including myself feel attached to the community surrounding the school
☐Strongly agree ☐Agree ☐Disagree ☐Strongly disagree

4–15. Teachers including myself think that they have to work hard for students at this school
☐Strongly agree ☐Agree ☐Disagree ☐Strongly disagree

4–16. Teachers including myself think that they have to listen to what school communities say
☐Strongly agree ☐Agree ☐Disagree ☐Strongly disagree

4–17. Teachers including myself consult with school communities when teachers have concerns over students' development and their learning
☐Strongly agree ☐Agree ☐Disagree ☐Strongly disagree

4–18. Teachers including myself think that they have to improve students' academic performance at this school
☐Strongly agree ☐Agree ☐Disagree ☐Strongly disagree

Appendix 3: Headteacher additional questionnaire

Date of filling in the sheet: _____

Name of school: _____

Name of person and title who filled in the sheet: _____

Please pick(✓) from the list below the <u>five (5) major community that feed students to your school</u>.

- The information of the listed community are from the Population and Housing Census 2010.
- If you identify relevant community as feeding one but the name is slightly different from listed one, please select those that are almost identical in terms of the community name.
- If they are not listed, please select the closest in terms of geographical locations.
- If feeding community are less than five, it is Ok for you to tick less than five.
- For example, if you identify ADEHETA is one of major feeding community to your school, tick like below.

✓ *ADEHETA*

Name of Community

ADEHETA	AVASHIVE
ADETSEWUI (AGBAKOPE)	AVEDO
ADRAKPO-AGBONYEMITSIKOPE	AVENORPEDO
ADZIKAME	AVENORPEME
AFATSAGBELEVE	AWANYAKOPE
AGBAFLOME	AYITIKOPE
AGBAGBLAKOPE	BAYIVE
AGBANUKOPE	DAGBAMATE
AGBEDRAFOR	DAWLO

(Continued)

(Continued)

Name of Community

AGORDOE	DZOGADZE
AGORNU-KPORKPLOTE	DZRAKATE
AGORWEME DUGA	DZUEPE/ATSIAME
AGORWEME-HOMADZIKOPE	FIATO/LEKETE/NYIDIKUKOPE
AGOVE	FIATO-GAMORKOPE
AHLIHADZI	GEFIA
AKATSI	GELIKOPE
AKEVE DAVORKOPE	GOKUKOPE
AKUAVE	GORNIKOPE
ALOKPA	GUIGA
ALORSEKOPE	GYAVE
AMEVUVORKOPE	HAVE
APEYIME	HAVEDZI
ATIDZIVE	HETORLOGO
ATSIEKPUI	HODZIKOPE
AVADRE	HORTI
KLOKPE	NKPOKOPE
KPEDATORKOPE	NOGOKPO
KPEGLOKOPE (ABLORKPO)	NYITAWUTA
KPELIKOPE	NYOGBORTE-ANYIHEME
KPODZIVI	NYORGBOR ANYIDZIME
KPOHE	SAKPAKUKOPE
KPOTA-KPOHE	SESIME
KUTSIME ESUSUKOPE	SREMANU
KWEGBAGA	SUIPEGA
KWEGBAGLIKPOME	TETEMALE
LAWUI-APEYIAME	TOGODO
LAWUI-AVEDZI	TORGBOKOPE
LIGIKOPE	TORVE
LIVEGA	TOVI
LOGAKOPE	TSIEVE
LOGOTE	TSIGBENE
LOKOKOPE	TUMAWUKOPE
LUME-AHUGAKOPE	WLITEY
LUME-AVETE	WUTE
MAMEDO	WUXOR
MONOME-ATIATE	XAVI
MORYIGA	YALUVI-DZOTSIKOPE
NGBLEBI	ZUTAGA

Appendix 4: Records of SMC or PTA executive or general meetings

	Code in the text	Date	Meeting title
1	A20160520	2015/5/20	CTA (Community, Teachers Association) meeting for the term three
2	A20160129	2016/1/29	CTA (Community, Teachers Association) general meeting
3	A20161019	2016/10/19	CTA (Community, Teachers Association) meeting for the first term in 2016/2017 academic year
4	A20170228	2017/2/28	CTA (Community, Teachers Association) meeting
5	A20170530	2017/5/30	CTA (Community, Teachers Association) meeting
6	A20170928	2017/9/28	CTA meeting
7	A201802	2018/2/1	CTA meeting
8	A20180518	2018/5/18	CTA meeting
9	B20120517	2012/5/17	3rd term PTA general meeting
10	B20120926	2012/9/26	1st term PTA general meeting
11	B20140212	2014/2/12	2nd term PTA general meeting
12	B20151013	2015/10/13	1st term PTA general meeting
13	B20161007	2016/10/7	1st term PTA general meeting
14	C20161111	2016/11/11	SMC/PTA general meeting
15	C20170724	July 24, 2016 or 2017 (the year is not visible, thus it is the author's guess)	PTA general meeting
16	D20110811	2011/8/11	PTA general meeting
17	D20131031	2013/10/31	PTA general meeting
18	D20140604	2014/6/4	PTA general meeting
19	D20141119	2014/11/19	PTA general meeting
20	D20150611	2015/6/11	PTA general meeting (to be assumed)
21	D20151029	2015/10/29	PTA meeting
22	D20160226	2016/2/26	PTA meeting
23	D20160609	2016/6/9	PTA meeting
24	D20161011	2016/10/11	PTA/SMC executive meeting

Appendix 5: Factor analysis of relational trust

	Item	Average	SD
	School communities-School relational trust	10.8	2.25
	Expectation factor	3.00	.41
SC12	School community understand concerns by the school about students' development and their learning	3.00	.58
SC10	School communities pay serious attention to whatever the school informs them of what happened to as well as what will be necessary for the school and students	2.84	.74
SC11	School communities participate in SMC or PTA general meetings actively	2.95	.65
SC9	School communities consult with the school when they have concerns about students and their education	3.12	.58
SC14	Teachers including myself feel attached to the community surrounding the school	3.27	.61
SC5	School communities provide necessary support for students' development and learning at the school	2.87	.72
SC7	School communities provide necessary support for teachers	2.54	.76
SC13	Talking with school communities help the school (headteacher and teachers) to understand them better	3.36	.53
	Obligation factor		
SC18	Teachers including myself think that they have to improve students' academic performance at this school	3.76	.50
SC15	Teachers including myself think that they have to work hard for students at this school	3.74	.44
SC17	Teachers including myself consult with school communities when teachers have concerns over students' development and their learning	3.52	.57
SC19	Teachers make best use of instructional hours to improve students' learning	3.54	.53
SC20	Teachers will conduct extra classes if school communities or parents request them to do so.	3.31	.68
	Headteacher-Teacher relational trust	12.36	2.4
	Expectation factors	3.49	.38
HTR3	Teachers make best use of instructional hours to improve students' learning	3.53	.50
HTR4	Teachers work hard to improve students' academic performance of this school	3.64	.48
HTR1	I count on teachers' capabilities to conduct their expected duties	3.57	.50
HTR2	Teachers come to school without delay or absence	3.28	.55
HTR5	Teachers share with each other their experience and what they have learned inside and outside the school	3.42	.50

Item		Average	SD
Obligation factor			
HTR10	I care about teachers' personal welfare	3.52	.67
HTR6	I support teachers' professional development	3.62	.49
HTR11	I appeal to local stakeholders (school communities, district education office, DA) if teachers need any support for their improved teaching and learning	3.44	.52
HTR9	I am pleased that teachers consult with headteacher over their concerns	3.48	.55

Appendix 6: Descriptive statistics of relational trust

Item		Average	SD
Teacher-Parent relational trust		9.62	2.49
Expectation factor		2.8	0.51
TPR4	Parents make sure that children come to school without any delay or absence	2.61	.76
TPR1	Parents provide necessary items (educational materials, school uniform, shoes etc.) for their children's development and education at the school	2.97	.59
TPR3	Parents provide breakfast for children to let them be active for school activities	2.73	.73
TPR2	Parents look after children's homework at home or secure their learning time at home	2.4	.76
TPR6	Parents pay serious attention to whatever the school inform parents of what happened to as well as what will be necessary for the school and students	2.81	.61
TPR5	Parents consult with teachers when parents have concerns about children and their education	3.01	.61
TPR7	Teachers feel a sense of familiarity with parents of this school	3.08	.54
Obligation factor		3.46	.33
TPR9	Teachers think that they have to work hard for students of this school	3.62	.56
TPR11	Teachers think that they have to improve students' academic performance of this school	3.73	.45
TPR13	Teachers think that they have to improve students' discipline of this school	3.68	.49
TPR10	Teachers think that they have to listen to what parents of this school say	2.98	.57
TPR12	Teachers think that they have to improve extra-curricular activities of this school	3.36	.55

(*Continued*)

(Continued)

	Item	Average	SD
TPR14	Teachers invite parents and students to school or visit them at home when teachers have concerns about students' development and learning	3.35	.50
TPR8	Talking with parents help teachers to understand parents and their children better	3.45	.65
	Teacher-Teacher relational trust	3.41	.38
	"Sharing each other" factor		
TTR5	Teachers share with each other anything they learned at training/workshop outside the school	3.51	.53
TTR4	Teachers feel that they can learn more from peer teachers at this school in terms of enhancing their expertise as teaching professionals	3.41	.54
TTR6	Teachers aim at enhancing their expertise as teaching professionals through training/workshop outside school	3.38	.53
TTR8	Teachers share and discuss with each other students' development and academic performance	3.57	.50
TTR7	Teachers share with each other their concerns and problems regarding pedagogical instructions	3.29	.48
	"Feeling comfortable" factor		
TTR1	It is OK at this school to discuss feelings, worries, and frustrations with other teachers	3.31	.51
TTR2	Teachers feel comfortable for asking questions to each other	3.38	.53
TTR3	Teachers feel comfortable for supporting each other	3.42	.52

Appendix 7: Descriptive statistics and correlation table (educational outcomes, community participation, socioeconomic status, and RT)

	Obs	Mean	SD	1	2	3	4	5	6	7	8	9
1. BECE mean aggregate (2017)	39	33.12	6.47		-3.19	-.413*	-.472	-.263	-.222	-.471**	-.095	-.146
2. Enrollment (Primary section) in 2016	78	147.10	112.69	-.319		-.525**	.503**	.079	-.177	.095	.132	.215
3. SES composite	50	0	1.000	-.413	-.525**		.385	.089	-.072	.164	.053	.133
4. Collective participation composite	36	0	1.000	-.472	.503**	.385		.227	.372*	.300	.056	.195
5. Relational trust composite	84	0	1.000	-.263	.079	.089	.227		.802**	.798**	.845**	.812**
6. School communities-school relational trust	85	10.80	2.25	-.222	-.177	-.072	.372*	.802**		.651**	.506**	.475**
7. Teacher-parent relational trust	85	9.62	2.53	-.471**	.095	.164	.300	.798**	.651**		.512**	.470**
8. Headteacher-teacher relational trust	84	12.36	2.4	-.095	.132	.053	.056	.845**	.506**	.512**		.717**
9. Teacher-teacher relational trust	85	3.41	0.38	-.146	.215	.133	.195	.812**	.475**	.470**	.717**	

Note: ** $p < 0.01$ * $p < 0.05$

Index

Note: Page numbers in *italics* indicate a figure and page numbers in **bold** indicate a table on the corresponding page.

For Product Safety Concerns and Information please contact our EU
representative GPSR@taylorandfrancis.com
Taylor & Francis Verlag GmbH, Kaufingerstraße 24, 80331 München, Germany

www.ingramcontent.com/pod-product-compliance
Lightning Source LLC
Chambersburg PA
CBHW061740270326
41928CB00011B/2319